TOUGH ROADS CREATE TOUGH PEOPLE
– VOL. 2

Anita Duckworth-Bradshaw

author**HOUSE**®

AuthorHouse™ UK
1663 Liberty Drive
Bloomington, IN 47403 USA
www.authorhouse.co.uk
Phone: UK TFN: 0800 0148641 (Toll Free inside the UK)
       UK Local: 02036 956322 (+44 20 3695 6322 from outside the UK)

© 2020 Anita Duckworth-Bradshaw. All rights reserved.

No part of this book may be reproduced, stored in a retrieval system, or transmitted by any means without the written permission of the author.

Published by AuthorHouse 08/27/2020

ISBN: 978-1-7283-5568-9 (sc)
ISBN: 978-1-7283-5569-6 (hc)
ISBN: 978-1-7283-5567-2 (e)

Print information available on the last page.

Any people depicted in stock imagery provided by Getty Images are models, and such images are being used for illustrative purposes only.
Certain stock imagery © Getty Images.

This book is printed on acid-free paper.

Because of the dynamic nature of the Internet, any web addresses or links contained in this book may have changed since publication and may no longer be valid. The views expressed in this work are solely those of the author and do not necessarily reflect the views of the publisher, and the publisher hereby disclaims any responsibility for them.

DEDICATION

To the men and women of the Powerhouse Global community, this book is for you. Thank you for your support of the Powerhouse Global Vision and Mission.

To my co-authors (Alexandra N'Ganga, Amina Leelo, Agnes George, Andrea Campbell, Bolatito Ayoola, Diane Curley, Caroline Emile, Elizabeth Lucas-Afolalu, Izabella Niewiadomska, Kevin Hill, Naoka Ito, Omita Gaikwad, Sabrina Nelson, Sandi Saksena and Verica Petrova); you are highly appreciated for travelling with me, and supporting this project. Your contributions are the reason for the success of this project. I thank you.

    *** **This book contains both British and American English. This is to keep the original writing of each contributor.** ***

CONTENTS

Chapter 1   "Through Hardships to the Stars"..................1
Chapter 2   Don't Let Anything Stop You 10
Chapter 3   Lessons from the Beautiful Game 24
Chapter 4   Tomorrow is not promised 38
Chapter 5   The Journey.. 46
Chapter 6   Together on The Far Side of Exhaustion 55
Chapter 7   Life Will Never Be The Same 72
Chapter 8   Strength and Wisdom From Life Experience...81
Chapter 9   Lessons from Jim Rohn................................97
Chapter 10 # Warning This Chapter Contains "Triggers"#......... 115
Chapter 11 Awakening Through Adversity..................129
Chapter 12 "Self-Worth Leads To Self-Love" 144
Chapter 13 Intent and Belief 156
Chapter 14 My Fight of Freedom 167
Chapter 15 Australia – Dreams, Decisions, Destination............. 173
Chapter 16 Global Visibility.......................................183

INTRODUCTION

Tough Roads Create Tough People – Vol.2 is a part series of a seven volumes global book project, aimed at showcasing some of the challenges and victories of global leaders. This project will provoke readers to take steps toward achieving their personal and business goals.

This book teaches us the importance of staying focused on our journey, and also to understand that everyone faces challenges at one point or another. Also, it reminds us that challenges helps build our mental muscles and helps us to become better humans.

"Tough Roads Create Tough People" – Anita Duckworth-Bradshaw

This book is a collective effort of high profile professionals who besides all their successful achievements, decided to share their stories and insights in various topics with the world through this book. They have gone the extra mile to offer some powerful practical tips on several different topics, which will eliminate the thought of 'self-doubt' and promote positive attitude towards greatness.

These professionals are located in different continents of the world, and each of their chapter is loaded with information that would transform your life.

CHAPTER 1

PER ASPERA AD ASTRA "THROUGH HARDSHIPS TO THE STARS"

by Amina Leelo

I was born as an Aquarius in the middle of the coldest winter in the land of the Northern Star into a Christian (Lutheran) family. From an early age my life has been filled with a love of music, as my father was a composer. In my childhood I was always a bit different and lived in my own world. I felt loneliness.

As a teenager, I had a lot of written correspondence with many teenagers from around the world. I loved to write letters to pen pals talking about my life and I was so excited to receive letters with interesting stories and photos from the other teenagers around the world. Not forgetting the exotic stamps on the envelopes, I received, which each had an interesting story of their own.

This was the time without smart phones and computers where one would express oneself through handwritten letters and photos. I loved that time! Being in contact with all these wonderful pen pals, I didn't feel loneliness anymore! When I look back to this time, it was a real connection time.

It was nice to write letters with different pens and trying to have nice handwriting. Today we are so used to typing our letters and then signing with our hand written signatures.

It was through the many pen pals from so many countries around the world that made me love our colourful Planet Earth and inspired me to want to see all the beautiful countries and learn many different languages. It also gave me a good chance to learn about other cultures and traditions!

When I was growing up, I started to travel and visit all these countries where my friends lived. I really enjoyed travelling and many times I travelled alone, as I loved my own peaceful space to explore every country not as an ordinary tourist, but I wanted to get to the roots of the country, people, culture and traditions I visited. I loved every country I visited as every country has its own unique people, culture and beauty.

Time passed by, I got married, gave birth to my 2 sons. got divorced, raised my sons to be educated and to be cosmopolitans, to respect and value people from all the different nationalities, cultures, and backgrounds. I wanted them to be able to speak many languages. I did manage to succeed in all this. I raised sons who respect all human beings and who can speak many languages.

One day it was time for me to understand that my sons were grown-ups and they wanted to get on with their own lives. My eldest son got married to a beautiful girl from India and my youngest decided to move into his own apartment. It was a big shock for me as my life was focused only on my sons. I did not know how to continue, how to get on with my own life not having them beside me all the time.

I started to search within myself and what goals I wanted in my life. I travelled alone to many places searching for myself, and the goals I wanted in my life. I travelled to Greece, where I spoke to a Greek Orthodox Priest for a long time under an orange tree. I travelled to the Vatican City in Italy, hoping to find my connection over there, but no, it was not meant for me. I travelled to India, but I didn't find what I was searching for their either, however I learned from this trip that you can be the happiest person in the world even when you don't have very much.

India was for me a great turning point. While I was raised in a country, where you take all things for granted – home, food etc. I saw the real life in India, where neighbours helped each other, where they lived in harmony with each other even though neighbours were from different religions. One neighbour was Hindu, another Muslim and another Christian, there was no difference! All of them respected and helped each other. Being kind to each other! One day some of the neighbours cooked and shared it with others... and the next day other neighbours did the same.

People had hardly anything, but they shared what they had and cared about each other and always had a beautiful smile on their faces. They were always there for each other!

All this goodness reflected my life a lot and I started to understand that we don't need much. Being good to each other, this is our richness! Caring, helping each other, this is what is most important.

Meanwhile during all this period, I was reading a lot about different religions. Somehow when I started to focus on reading about Islam, I felt the logics of this religion was very close and understandable for me. I started to focus more on reading about this religion and I ended up listening to a Quran reciting. I did not understand Arabic at this time at all, but there was something which found its way into my heart and I felt that I wanted to become a Muslim. I did not know any Muslims at this time, so I got all my information about Islam from the internet.

I learned the opening chapter of the Qur'an and some other short chapters by heart and started to pray.

One day I decided to go to my nearest Islamic centre in Finland, to check if it was possible to take some classes there. I was very excited to go there the first time as it was my first real meeting with other Muslims. I was welcomed by some Sheikh there, who was originally from Somalia. My first feeling of excitement quickly changed to a huge disappointment as the person of this Islamic centre was not the best representative of Islam. I left this place pretty quickly and decided not to search for any other Islamic centre in Finland but to travel to some Islamic country to get more knowledge about Islam.

I have to mention here about my first connection with Bahrain!

My very first visit to Bahrain was really by chance! I had a four-hour stopover in the kingdom. At the time my knowledge about Bahrain was very limited, so to get to know the place I decided to take a quick tour, grabbed a taxi from the airport and drove around. I do not know what happened exactly, but I definitely fell in love with the country from the first moment I landed. I deeply felt that it was a place where I would love to return and stay for a while where I could get to know this beautiful country and get more knowledge about Islam!

I fulfilled my dream and returned to Bahrain in August 2009 for one month as I decided that this would be the place for me to get more knowledge about Islam.

I arrived in Bahrain and to be honest, I did not know anybody in Bahrain. Somehow, I had a good feeling and strong trust for this country.

I felt secure to walk and drive alone as a woman in Bahrain. Nobody ever disturbed me. The only thing that happened, was that the local people stopped me and asked if I needed any help. It was something totally new for me!

I became a Muslim just one day before Ramadan and started my first ever fasting as a Muslim in my life. I was a bit worried how I would manage, as my mornings always started with drinking water and coffee.

Fasting was much easier than I expected, and my first Ramadan passed by very quickly!

When Ramadan was over I felt I knew almost all the people of Bahrain as during Ramadan time I got acquainted with so many nice people who invited me to their homes for Iftar and took care that I had all and everything I needed.

My one month passed by too quickly and when it was time to travel back home, I felt, that I couldn't leave this beautiful island. The hospitality of Bahrainis people, their caring and generous souls, welcoming open arms, especially towards guests and their big hearts is enormous and irresistibly. I felt this is my place where I want to stay!

I took a decision to prepare for my move to Bahrain and I returned back home to finalise everything over there. When I returned to Bahrain in

October and the new page of my life began. It is now the eleventh year I am living here on this land of the Two Seas and I have loved every single day living here.

When I returned to Bahrain, I became a local tourist guide as I loved to show the beauty of this country to all the other guests who came to visit this island. The beautiful Land of the Two-Seas drew me to become deeply attached to the island. From that moment onwards I had an urge to tell the whole world what a beautifully diversified country Bahrain is! It was like I started a beloved mission; to share my story about Bahrain with the rest of the world and tell a tale that has flourishing details in every single page. To make my dream become true, I established my own company and called it Stella Polare Boutique Events.

The name Stella Polare means a Northern Star which is famous for staying still in the sky while at the same time the entire northern sky is moving around it. That is because it's uniquely located close to the north celestial pole, the point around which the entire northern sky is turning. The reason Polaris is so important is because the axis of Earth is pointed almost directly at it. During the course of the night, Polaris does not rise or set, magically though it remains nearly at the same spot above the northern horizon year-round while the other stars are circling around it.

England's national poet and famous playwright, Shakespeare made a reference to it in his quote "I am constant as the northern star."

I truly hope Stella Polare Boutique Events will have an abundance of bright light to connect Bahrain with all the world and to globally reach every single spot in order to open unlimited channels of connection and communication while unleashing many opportunities.

I started to organise events in Bahrain and international events outside of the country and have had four successful events in Finland. On my last event in Finland we had a group of Bahraini ladies talking about the status of women in Bahrain and GCC. I did not expect that this would be such an interesting topic for the Finnish audience, as the thinking about the women in the Gulf was very different from the reality.

From this event I understood that I have to organise more events with and for women to bring more awareness about each other, to know each other better, to understand each other, to learn from each other, and to inspire, motivate and support each other. By understanding and supporting each other we can make this world a much better place to live!

I established Stella Women Around the World organization. My first event totally about women was held in Estonia, Tallinn in March 2019. We had a group of fifteen ladies from Bahrain and one lady from Saudi Arabia representing the Gulf region. There were three topics on our symposium – Women in Three religions, Women in Crises & Women as Entrepreneurs. The event was a huge success and it proved to me that these events for women are so needed and should go on every year in a different country to involve more ladies.

Following on from this I started to prepare a new event – International Conference "Women in Innovation & Creativity Globally" in Bahrain, hotel Sofitel in March 25.-29,2020. There was immense interest and I had over 100 ladies joining this event from outside the Gulf region from 40 different countries all around the world. We prepared a unique international program with a 2-day Conference, a Fashion Show and a Gala Concert. All of us were so excited about this upcoming event and we were counting the days for the event to begin.

But what happened next was that Covid-19 destroyed all our plans. Our long- awaited event was postponed to September 16.-20,2020. It was shocking news to all of us. Especially at the beginning, as it seemed not possible what was happening in our lives! All countries closed their borders and all the people got stuck in their homes. Many businesses got hit from this lock down very hard and many people lost their jobs, many people got sick, many people recovered, and some people did not make it.

COVID-19 pandemic has completely changed our lives. Here we see how quickly all can change. We never know what can be next.

Now living over four months with this virus, I think we all have learned a lot! The most important message is for all of us – never take anything for granted.

I can also find many good points from this hard time.

Suddenly we all got **TIME.**

Time to notice that Nature is sending us a message! We must take care about the nature as the past has shown what disasters have happened due to the wrong behaviour of the human beings. During the lockdown, our Planet Earth become more cleaner when the people stayed home.

We got time to think, time to listen, time to spend with our families, time to organise many things we had no time to do before.

Time to become a better person. Time to ask forgiveness from the people we have offended. Time to care about each other. Time to drop arrogance. Time to drop jealousy. Time to drop envy.

Time to unite and stop hater for the religion, skin colour.

Time to LOVE each other and do all to make this World a much better place, where we can live in harmony **ALL TOGETHER!**

"A rough road leads to the stars"

My Social Media links:

Stella Polare Boutique Events Website: www.stellapolarevents.com
Stella Women Around the World Website: www.stellawomenaroundtheworld.com
Instagram: https://www.linkedin.com/in/amina-l-alghamdi-407a1499/
https://www.linkedin.com/company/stella-polare-boutique-events/
Twitter: @stellapolarebh
Instagram: stellapolarebh
Facebook: https://web.facebook.com/stellapolarebh/
https://web.facebook.com/profile.php?id=100040622051712

CHAPTER 2

DON'T LET ANYTHING STOP YOU

By Alexandra N'Ganga – Founder and CEO of Aullyn

*To my supportive family and friends,
my coaches and mentors, my fellow entrepreneurs
and my inspiring clients,
Thank you.*

Introduction

The road to success is tough and, at times, lonelier than you can ever imagine. In my business journey, I won, I learned, I cried, and I rejoiced… But despite this bumpy road I wouldn't change a thing. Reflecting on my life a few times and considering my evolution of these last few years as an entrepreneur, I feel that this chapter is my greatest opportunity to share, for the first time, my journey of transformation. I wish it helps someone to not give up and pursue his/her divine path with faith.

I evolved from being a dreamer who managed to create, what is today, a well-known product for women with curly and afro hair, into a growth driven entrepreneur and business mentor. I saw how crucial it is to have a map, to have clarity on my plans and be purposeful. Write your goals down on paper, it becomes reality. Equally, the writing process of this chapter made it even more clear to me which way I need to go to in the coming years. When writing out a strategy, there is no space in lacking confidence nor courage. As an entrepreneur and a business mentor I am cause and consequence. In a short period of time I realized that working on my business is an important chapter, but working on myself is a lifelong learning process which has benefited me so far and, in case you're doubting, I can promise you it will benefit you too.

So, how did it all happen? What have I learned? Where did my focus go? Why did I struggle? How did I bridge the gap between my past and present situation? I will tell you all about it in the next paragraphs. But, first allow me to tell you about myself.

I was always a Leader

I am Alexandra, a people-oriented person. I am the founder and CEO of Aullyn which helps women gain time in their beauty ritual with combined hair products and I am a business mentor. I live in Brussels, Belgium since 2010. My husband and I have two lovely daughters, Sara (6) and Melinda (3). As a multi passionate entrepreneur, I wake up every day excited about helping consultants, coaches and business owners to level up their business. Through my Facebook group *Business Mentoring Daily* I give them all the necessary tools they can apply instantly to see significant results in their venture.

I am the second child of five siblings. My parents moved from Congo-Brazzaville to France in 1981 when my older brother was 2 years old. In August 1983, I see the light and few years later, I welcome two other brothers in 1986 and 1991. My biggest wish was to have a sister and finally in 1992, my sister and partner in business Christye joins the family. Our parents raised us in respect of the Christian values and taught us to work hard. At a very young age I was given several responsibilities and always trusted by my parents to be the one in charge in their absence. I think that my upbringing made me a leader; for sure, it has played a big role in my willingness to become an entrepreneur.

Anita Duckworth-Bradshaw

The creation of Aullyn

Time with your loved ones is precious

Back in 2005, after three years in University in Paris, I started to feel the need to take a break from studying. I wanted more concrete learnings. Young, confident, and with my parents' agreement, I took the opportunity to move to a friend's house in the UK with the goal to explore professional possibilities and improve my English. Only one condition to that plan: finish University and obtain my diploma, when I return. After eighteen months between Birmingham and London, in September 2006, I had to rush back home: our youngest brother Johann, aged 15, had been feeling unwell some days before, but doctors couldn't give a clear diagnosis. When my parents said his state improved a little, I thought I could book a return ticket with ease. Unfortunately, things happened fast, in a way we couldn't control. Johann died on September 9th, 2006 and I wasn't next to him in his last moments. I returned to Paris and grieved with my family. I am unable to describe the pain we went through. Our hearts are broken, and the memories is all that we have now. Time is our most precious resource and I understood that the hard way. This event changed my relationship to people and time forever.

Helping other women juggling with several responsibilities

In 2013, when my first daughter Sara was born, spending as much time as possible with her was my priority. I enjoyed it greatly in the first three months but very quickly combining breastfeeding, work, personal care and everyday life commitments made it impossible to create some free time for me. I had to change to infant formula earlier than planned due to stress and felt depressed to have given up on that special moment with my daughter. You're probably wondering what is the link with hair products? Well, many women lack the time and energy to care for themselves and their hair especially. In a society where hair is an important part of the definition of beauty and self-confidence, my pain was louder day after day. I wanted to feel great and look fabulous. I wanted to have the beautiful results with high quality products, but I had a limited time. Often, (black) women leave hair care to the back burner because it takes easily two to three hours from shampooing to a finished hairstyle. As a consequence, if you're a woman with a busy schedule, and you have a little time to rest between work, house chores and kids, you'd probably decide not to do certain things and in my case, it was feeling pain in my arms as I spent time on my hair to be detangled and nourished.

Few months down the line, when Sara was 8 months, I had lost so much volume on my head due to dryness, breakage, and fatigue that I asked my sister for help. Christye is, what we call, a Nappy, a woman of African heritage, embracing the beauty of her natural afro hair and aware of its specific needs. The Nappy movement started in the USA about twenty years ago and since then emerged in Europe, Africa, South America and the rest of the world. With that, a new market arose where experts hairstylists, doctors, bloggers travel around the world and get paid to share their best natural hair care practice and encourage women to love their hair (as opposed to preferring chemically straightening solutions a.k.a perm or relaxer). In 2014, my sister and I decide to attend a yearly educational event – Natural Hair Academy Paris - for women with afro hair. After sharing my struggle with other attendees that day, I realized that many other women considered it a pain spending more time than they wanted doing their haircare routine. Because, in reality it meant spending time away from what matters the most to them.

I have always loved management and business in general, which I studied in University. So, at that moment my creative mind and 'solution-for-all' mentality started to focus on alleviating the overwhelm that busy women, like me, could feel daily. On that specific day, I knew that I would be offering my products in the next Natural Hair Academy show in March 2015. And we did. My sister jumped with me in this adventure and our brand Aullyn was on the market, in time to present the first four products we imagined facilitating women's life*: "fast and natural care, merging 2 functions in 1 to save your time".*

My tough road

The setbacks

In the first three years, we managed to create partnerships in the Caribbean, in Africa, Spain, France and Benelux. Next to that we adjusted our sales strategy and focused on expanding our online presence. Our sales were rising and our products very appreciated. The time I saved from my haircare routine seemed to be reinvested in this venture which I gave all my energy, after my family and my 9 to 5 job. As we got more and more popular, I started to think of leaving my regular job, but some real challenges came in the way of that dream. Our market is promising yet achieving financial independence is a matter of mindset which I didn't know back then. I used to be a dreamer, a woman who wanted to create the best solution so that women could win their time back and have more freedom. I would poorly delegate and only trust my sister to work with me. Making a lot of money was a byproduct of my plan. I wanted to be busy helping others, but I didn't know what running a business meant. Our customers were happy, but we the financial reward of our hustle was limited. I emptied my cup, my sister's cup and one day, in June 2018, she announced to me that she needed some time off to focus on her personal goals. My sister is my best friend and it took me several weeks to accept her choice. I couldn't help but think I was responsible for it. Without her I started to feel insecure, overwhelmed and the reason why I started Aullyn seemed to fade in the mix of my feelings.

Two months later, more bad news hit me. My husband, who always worked as a diplomat, saw his contract stopped without notice. This is something most people can't understand if they don't know this domain. We always knew it could happen, but we weren't ready for it at that moment. With that, another stress added to the picture and my dream to become a full time CEO moved further away. It is my duty to care for my family with my stable income…my 9 to 5. My husband is a strong and positive man, but this setback took him into worries and naturally both of us had to work harder to manage our emotions. Through this challenge, I was convinced that we would eventually be victorious, but I didn't know when… "God, why me? Why us?" How long would our faith be tested? "God, what are you wanting to achieve in my life with this situation?". What I didn't realize then is that this time of our life was the challenge I needed to become the woman I am today.

Climbing out of the dark zone

Sorrow, anger, fatigue, depression sound great when you play the role of the victim, but it doesn't pay. With nobody to turn to, I decided that I will be the rock I have always been, I will sort things out myself. I will fight. No help, no pity required. I started to speak to myself in these terms, but the truth was I wanted to scream "Help me please" because I realized I had no control on things. It was an emotional rollercoaster.

The first coach I worked with in 2018, Stella Bida, an International Speaker and Success Strategist taught me that branding, marketing and networking are keys to success. At that time, with less money and no real confidence on what I had to do, I knew the best thing I could do was expand my network and socialize more, go to events with the goal to make my brand more known. This is how I met another businesswoman Yadira Gonzalez Muñoz who became a friend. She could understand my challenges without judging me and that's all we, human beings, need sometimes: understanding of our emotions. Yadira's personal journey reminded me that our challenges are teachings. She shared with me how, in 2010, she had been a victim of a car accident with her kids. All of them survived the crash but she had been the most injured. The doctors placed her in a coma for days and when she woke up, one of them announced to her she would never walk again…And here she was, standing in front of me in November 2018, telling me about God's miracle; that her strong will and prayers to the Lord Jesus are what gave her the strength to fight. As a Christian, this resonated greatly with me. I believe that God's plan is perfect, yet instead of letting Him conduct my life, I was trying too hard to be in control by any means. I didn't want to ask for help but God sent me a helper because I needed one. Yadira convinced me to go to the 4-day training of Peak Performance Coach Tony Robbins "Unleash the power within" in London. Yes indeed, it is what you think! For four days, I screamed, jumped, cried along with eleven thousand people and learned enormously about human psychology and myself. I walked on hot coals, just like Oprah Winfrey did. It was a life changing experience. The fear, the doubts, the lack of confidence vanished, and I came back to Belgium changed forever.

Months before this event, I had committed to grow spiritually too and increase my understanding of the Bible. Being more aware of God's word led me to get baptized publicly in March 2019. I acknowledged my identity: I am the daughter of the highest power that exists. God loves me (and loves you too!). From that moment onwards, all my personal and business plans became obvious. My plans are God's plans. I know what you're thinking now, it doesn't say much, but wait…What I'm sharing with you here is crucial, it is the turning point of personal growth. When you understand that you are the piece of a divine plan, that you are an individual with a life purpose, that you are here on Earth for a reason, your real focus becomes fulfilment of your mission not money or people's judgement. Your quest is to discover what your purpose is. Thinking back about the time my sister left our business, I understood that our life purpose is just different, and she did what was right for her. She remains close to me as an advisor and she is destined to win on her own professional path.

Life will never be the same again

Thanks to these experiences, I realized that I could go forward and be who I am and who I am meant to be. I am resilient, flexible and capable of achieving things beyond my imagination. Before that breakthrough, God was sitting on the passenger seat of my life and now God is driving my life and I sit on the passenger seat. I had a "nothing can stop me now" feeling and I could see clearly which way to go, which things to stop doing and where I could accelerate and grow. This feeling is contagious and until today I passed it on to all the people who needed to rebuild their confidence. People would then come to me and ask for my advice because I stand strong, confidently and conscious that I have work to do and proud of the lessons learned through my struggle. As the saying goes, "Every master was once a disaster". Quite reassuring, right!

The benefits of my Transformation

For the growth of Aullyn and myself

A business can only grow up to the abilities of its leader. This means that I have a fair share of responsibility for all things that happen, good or bad. It has been difficult to accept that I was the cause of my results, on top of the problems I had on my way. When you step in your leadership role fully, it spreads around you and you get more respect from your team and peers. People come to you, listen to you and you don't have to chase them. Your actions and results speak for you. From the moment I understood that, I made a complete shift and started to take massive actions on all aspects of my life. I adopted the following principles: always be a solution finder, don't make excuses, get the work done.

For my mentees

While continuing my own growth journey in business, I could recognize the same patterns occurring with other businesspeople. Whenever I speak on stage, I meet other entrepreneurs who share their concerns. I was more and more solicited to talk about how I handle my business growth and evolution. This triggered me in helping them in developing their business. I fulfil my role as a CEO and mentor other business owners to gain and maintain success. For sure, I am living on purpose and nothing compares to that. As often as I can remember, I make my clients and fellow business owners think out of the box and go for an internal journey to become better and more focused. I love to spread knowledge and see my clients grow in their field in a very autonomous way. This really makes me tick. Helping others is for me fuel for growth.

For my family and my kids in particular

I run all my activities while being a mother to two lovely girls. I love to take care of my children and am also eager to see them grow into confident women. I want to be a model for them. I have always been a project leader, so handling the household and parenting is management in a loving but organized way. I have three babysitters and ask for help when I need it. I work with several freelancers which allow me to delegate what isn't part of Aullyn's core business. My husband and our eldest accompany me in my dreams and aspirations for the future. Sara knows each product of our range and enjoys suggesting new ideas. I encourage her to be creative, I don't limit her, and I wish that my journey inspires them always to pursue their dreams and the path God created for them. Family is everything to me. When my second daughter was born in 2017, I felt good and more grounded. By becoming an entrepreneur, I learned to focus on the time I could offer myself and my family.

Five Keys to Successful Leadership

Have a plan

Plan with the end in mind. The plan is the road you create to get to your destination. You need to have a strategy, a written set of actions that you will evaluate, review and adapt. The key question is who does what and when. It's as simple as it is strategic, and it's essential to define this to be able to react and readjust your actions quickly. I often say that a CEO is a maestro who coordinates all the company's leaders (instruments) together. Beware then of false notes that can cost you money. You and your entire team must know what needs to be done and in what time frame.

Continuously grow by adding knowledge

I knew setting my mindset for success was my biggest mental challenge. Visualizing before something happens was impossible to me. The key to this blockage is education. Yes, as simple as that. No vision board, no affirmation, pick a good book written by an expert; the more knowledge you gain, the more possibilities you will envision. By dedicating yourself to learning, you can get ahead in every aspect of your life. All it takes is a commitment. I personally read one to two hours daily. I pick areas where I need to grow and do incremental changes consistently. I also follow online courses that can help me become more effective in getting the results I want for my business. Also, something that many entrepreneurs tend to forget is to keep learning about the changes happening in their field. Always be ready to change and adapt.

Choose a mentor

A couple of years ago, I had the opportunity to exchange few words with Kim Kiyosaki in London. With her husband Robert Kiyosaki, she specializes in Real Estate investments and financial education. I asked her the following question: "Kim, if you could give me one single piece of advice to accelerate my growth, what would it be?" and she said with a very caring voice "Find a mentor, someone who has succeeded where you want to succeed". The truth about business is that many people paved the way for us and success leaves clues; meaning that learning from the ones who have experience is the way forward, no need to reinvent the wheel. Follow the men and women who have spent years learning how to succeed ahead of you. Don't be afraid to ask people for their input and advice. Ask them for their guidance and ideas. If you follow famous businesspeople, you may not be able to ask them personally but make sure to read their books and articles or attend their live events. As a mentor, I am interested in helping entrepreneurs set the right foundations for their business because I know how strategic it is to set things right from the start.

Stay focused

Successful people focus on using every minute of their time to get maximum results. They are more productive than others because they adopt healthy habits in their business and their life. The more they get educated, the bigger their dreams. Also, they refuse to give time to things that take their focus away from their ultimate goals. If you're not satisfied by your results today, chances are that you need to focus more to get the job done. If you're a perfectionist like I used to be, you may be familiar with procrastination, this is not only the thief of time; it is the thief of life. Don't spend time comparing yourself with others. I used to find plenty of excuses because I was comparing myself to others: "They have older children, this is easier, they have more time" or "they have no kids, of course they have time to think". Well it is what it is, don't be a victim. I chose to have children, so I adapted my business management, delegated a lot of the work that I didn't have to do. I could feel the relief as I leveraged my time by releasing all the activities that weren't relevant for my business growth.

Never give up

This is my favourite part when I teach my clients about the success mindset and emotional intelligence. Most of the time, my clients don't realize how much strength and talents they have. Trust yourself and focus on the solutions you can find rather than the obstacles. Instead of asking "Why me?", I just look beyond the problem and rejoice about the growth behind the challenge. Remember that, despite the setbacks of life, and even though everyone around you is quitting and giving up on their dreams, there is almost always a solution. The key is to take constant action, massive action. Look at your goals every day, adapt your plan if needed and keep persisting until you make it. There are many obstacles on the road to success, but your job is to use them as stepping-stones and to persist until you succeed.

Conclusion

In my experience of entrepreneurship, there's nothing such as business issues. I would rather say that personal issues or lack of knowledge reflect on your business. My biggest issues were my emotions and how I used to manage them. When I decided I had enough of my sad self, it all changed! Yes, I got mad at myself for not rising up to my standards, for not showing my full potential. I owed it to myself, to my company, to the people who trusted me and supported me. Now, that you know my story, what will you do differently in your business? Are you facing challenges and think there is no way out? You are more than welcome to contact me if you're looking for help. In any case, wear your confidence hat even if you don't feel like it. Always be happy to help others, keep learning, don't isolate yourself. If your dream is worth fighting for, do whatever it takes and pray for it. God can do miracles if you believe in His power. In His time, you shall see your victory.

ABOUT THE AUTHOR

Alexandra N'Ganga is the founder and CEO of Aullyn Cosmetics and a business mentor. She helps entrepreneurs easily build a profitable business and achieve their personal. Through her first venture, Aullyn, she has been generating consistently 5 to 6-figure revenue every year for the last five years.

As a business mentor, she helps consultants, coaches and business owners set the right foundations for their businesses by providing step by step frameworks. She uses the latest tools and technologies to increase the sales and profits of her client's businesses.

Alexandra is also a speaker with a passion to inspire and empower leaders to pursue their dreams with faith. Her entrepreneurial journey to success is not only relatable but educative. She aims to help as many people as possible to have the right mindset and the right strategy to create the life they want.

Links

Aullyn: www.aullyncosmetics.com
Mentoring group: https://www.facebook.com/groups/bmdachievers/
Linkedin: www.linkedin.com/in/alexandra-n-st-germain

CHAPTER 3

LESSONS FROM THE BEAUTIFUL GAME

ANDREA CAMPBELL

This month marks 20 years since I lost my younger brother – Gary. He had been a seemingly healthy young man in the prime of his life, just embarking on his entrepreneurial journey. At 24 he was the first of my mother's five children to establish his own business - a driving school with a small fleet of second-hand cars. Gary was not an academic; rather, he was a practical person – wise beyond his years and promising. One autumn day he received a diagnosis of kidney failure and within a few weeks he was gone. I miss my brother and as I commemorate his loss I remember how he loved the beautiful game – football or soccer for some. And so, I thought it might be fitting to look at the many lessons that I have identified in this game and I invite you to join me on this personal, yet, engaging journey of exploration.

i) *Mission Statement* – Every professional football club has a mission statement defining the company's objectives and they share them with their players as part of their induction. The clubs document these governance statements and often display them prominently along with their vision, values and core beliefs. In our lives we too must have a mission. We must find our purpose and set out on a mission to achieve it, guided by our values, vision and core beliefs. Those who fail to find their purpose often fail to achieve their full potential. No amount of material gain will bring the level of fulfillment that is possible if we find the source of our difference and use that to make a difference in the world.

ii) *Drive* – Irrespective of a team's position in the league tables, they must maintain their drive. There is no shortage of takers for the position if a highly-placed team loses momentum resulting in a slip in its performance. Even when it is clear that a team will lose, a professional team must keep up the momentum, maintaining a positive attitude and giving all they've got. In life too we must maintain our drive – a persistence and determination to succeed. It is normal for us to get tired or to lose interest; we may even fall but we must pick ourselves up and get going again. If we are serious about achieving a goal we have to keep up the momentum; complacency is not an option. In every walk of life there are moments that we find difficult and may even feel unable to handle. Those moments washed with blood, sweat, or tears yet we must wrestle with the urges to quit. There is no shortage of tests – obstacles in our way that seek to deter us from achieving our goals. We must have the tenacity to do what it takes to overcome the barriers in our way. We cannot be afraid to reach out for help and tap into available sources, for pride has no place in the determination and will to succeed. We sometimes find ourselves stretched to capacity and just like in football; we often have to fill in the gaps despite our utter exhaustion. With a will and way however, we *live to see another day. And this goes on and on!*

iii) *Teamwork* – Football is a team game; no single individual on his own can make a team successful. A group of people come together to train, plan and execute; sometimes they win and sometimes they lose. The goals and resulting win are celebrated by all, not just by the individuals who were lucky enough to score. It is not unusual to see team members setting up goals for their colleagues to score. Poor team working has a negative impact on team morale and ultimately on the team's level of success. In the wider society we have to adopt an attitude of collaboration. This is not a new concept - countries form economic blocs, corporations merge or form strategic alliances, entrepreneurs form partnerships to optimize opportunities. *"No man is an island"*. We have to learn to work with people in order to pool and leverage our strengths for mutual benefit. We must therefore connect with each other to do more for self and others as we endeavor to leave a legacy in the world.

iv) *Communication* – Effective communication is vital if a team is to be successful. Communication isn't limited to verbal commands; gestures and movement can be just as effective for communicating on the field. Footballers point to spaces where they want the ball to be passed, they point out attackers that need to be marked and they undertake a range of motions with the aim of communicating with teammates and their manager. Communication has been a key structural element in every society since the beginning of time. It is the glue that holds everything together. Good communication is the basis of true and meaningful relationships. It is through communication that we share experiences, feelings, thoughts, and needs with others openly, honestly, directly, constructively, and non-judgmentally.

v) *Confidence* – In order to be successful, footballers have to be confident. It has to be a daunting experience to face thousands of fans who are expecting a win no matter what, but these men and women face their reality with confidence, knowing that they will do their best to bring joy to many. Even though they know that there will be moments when they lose, they endeavor to portray confidence and I have no doubt that some of them *fake it until they make it*. As we go about our professional and personal lives we often experience fear – a natural phenomenon and thief of potential. We fear failure, people's criticisms, inadequacy; we feel we are not qualified enough and we doubt our ability to succeed. Some people may not recognise your value but once you have undertaken the relevant preparation, dare to be confident irrespective of any issues - past or present - that you may have. Tell yourself that you are good enough. Beware of other people's insecurities and do not allow them to be a source of deterrence as you step boldly into your space.

vi) *Scoring* – The ultimate aim of a football team is to score more goals than the opponent and thus win the game. Team members are aware of the target and they know that there are obstacles in the way. They keep their eyes and minds focused, never losing sight of their target. We too should keep our eyes on our targets in order to be able to score in due season. We have to set goals and take steps to achieve them. When we go with the flow, life just floats along and without our sights on a set destination we end up some place someday, doing something with someone, not being sure of what that thing is. Though we may have to change the goalposts from time to time, it is important to set goals to help us chart our paths to our desired objective. We have to be clear on what we are aiming for, with a full knowledge of what we want, and why we want it. We have to know when we have achieved it, what would happen if we don't and importantly, what would happen if we do. Many of us have learnt to handle failure but we struggle with success. We can't afford to hit our target only to have it slip from our hands because we weren't prepared for it.

vii) *Forgiveness* – Individuals within a team often make mistakes that lead to the awarding of a penalty to the opposing side. Needless to say, a resulting goal is often the difference between winning and losing. This is painful but the team has to overcome the situation, acknowledge their loss as a team and not focus on the individual who committed the error. We too have to forgive and not allow ill feelings to fester. We have to look for the good in the person and not dwell on the offence. Forgiveness liberates; it is not about the other person being let off the hook, for that person will have to live with the consequences of his actions, forgiven or not. When we learn to forgive we free ourselves from inner turmoil. We give ourselves the opportunity to be happy again and embrace the possibility of leading a fulfilling and meaningful life.

viii) *Celebration of the small successes* - When a football game is in progress each goal is celebrated, even if there are 80 minutes left to play. Although the game is not over, the players, their management team and indeed their fans celebrate the successes along the way. Too often we think that we have to conquer the entire mountain before we dare to celebrate. We shouldn't be pessimistic and rigid. It is important to celebrate the small steps, for the big (often visible) achievements are made up of smaller (often invisible), consistent actions. Life is also about the moments of the journey, not just the final destination.

ix) *Time management* – Footballers have to turn up at predetermined times for their practice sessions and they have to commit an agreed number of hours to practicing. Time is a very important factor on the field – matches start at set times and players are expected to play for 90 minutes and extra time if necessary. Time is a great resource – not one to be wasted. There are many factors in today's society that can waste our time if not managed effectively – emails, chats, text, telephone calls, social and official functions, social visits, meetings, traffic etc. We have to identify the time wasters in our lives and manage them. Learn to identify those tasks that are important and urgent versus those that aren't. I have come to realize that some things, though they are important, have to wait. The gurus suggest the following ordered approach: Urgent and Important; Not Urgent but Important; Urgent but not Important, and finally - Neither Urgent nor Important. The biggest lesson here is the fact that time lost cannot be regained; use it wisely.

x) *Commitment and dedication* – Footballers generally earn significant sums and there are many who feel that they earn too much when compared with other professionals. What is often ignored is the level of commitment and dedication that they put into their preparation. While we are asleep or relaxing they have to get out of their beds at unsociable hours and face wind, rain and sun in order to meet their training targets. We too have to be committed and dedicated to whichever endeavour we undertake. We cannot run away *when the going gets rough* or when we *cannot see the wood for the trees*. We have to develop staying power and if we believe in what we do we'll stay and see it through. Aim for sustainability and longevity; if your venture eventually folds you'll have the courage to say in all honesty that you gave it a fair shot.

xi) *Strategy* – Even if, like me, you don't know much about football, you are likely to be able to recognise strategies on the field when you see it. The game follows key principles and formations i.e. strategies for which the team planned. If you fail to plan a strategy to achieve your goals they will remain as dreams, or may even turn into nightmares. If you just go with the flow, chances are you will wash up anywhere. While that may be acceptable to some people, most of us have to put strategies in place in order to survive and thrive. Turn your dreams into visions and face the future, armed with a strategy.

xii) *Staying calm under pressure* – This characteristic is shown particularly when players are taking penalties. There is tremendous pressure and the result of their effort may not reflect their level of skill. There are many things in life that put us under pressure – economics, politics, technology; the environment, social issues, ethical conflicts, among others. Our ability to remain calm reduces our stress level and strengthens our coping mechanism. There will always be hills and valleys in our path but we have to look beyond the immediate and recognise that there is always a way, even when we cannot see the way. Bear in mind that if we fail today, *tomorrow is another day* to try again.

xiii) *Resilience* – I have never seen a football game where all the players remain on their feet throughout. Invariably they are tripped or fall over from time to time but although they may hurt, they keep going. There are cases when they are injured and need medical attention but as long as they receive medical clearance they remain in action until they are substituted or the game is over. In life we will be hurt sometimes, knocked over - even trampled, we may be broke or broken and we may bleed but *once there's life, there's hope.* We will get hurt but we must not remain wounded. Get up and bounce back and finish your game! In life we will experience setbacks but see these as setups for your comeback. They are all part of the process – beautiful roses are completed through thorns. You owe it to yourself and to those who believe in you, to stay the course.

xiv) *Physical exercise and keeping fit* – Footballers have to be fit; they constantly exercise in order to be able to outmaneuver and outlast the competition. While some of us are physically unfit; what is important is that we endeavour to keep ourselves healthy to the best of our ability so that we give ourselves the best chance of success. Keeping fit includes avoiding excesses that harm our bodies and make us unable to fulfill our purpose. It encompasses deliberate actions to achieve balance and to seek help when required. It includes getting enough sleep and rest and feeding our mind, body and spirit.

xv) *Passion* – Those who play football are not only drawn to the high wages and fame – they generally have significant passion for the game. This is what makes them get out of bed early; it keeps them going even after they have made their millions. They are doing what they love to do and it may not even feel like work. We too must find the source of our passion and do what makes us happy. If we enjoy our work, we are more likely to turn up in the rain, wind and snow. We will be motivated and we will want to do it well. Passion gives us staying power which makes us tough and gives us that steely attitude *when the going gets rough.*

xvi) *Regard for family* – After a tournament players can often be seen relaxing in exotic places with their significant other. Good sportsmen spend time with their families; returning to basics for a dose of reality from time to time. They balance work life with family life, ensuring that neither suffers. Too many families fall apart because individuals within the family fail to make time for others. They are caught up in their own careers and they think that being able to shower their family with money and expensive gifts can replace quality time. Ultimately their personal lives suffer initiating a vicious cycle as their professional lives take a dive. Life is about balance – achieve the right balance and your happiness and success will be heightened.

xvii) *Flexibility* – Although the team plans a particular strategy with their manager, they often have to change, based on the actions of their opponents. We often see managers substituting players or we may see a change in strategy after half time. Players have to play in varying climatic conditions – they have to adapt. In life we too have to be flexible. Having a strategy is essential but as we do not exist in a vacuum we must bear in mind that the external environment will bring to bear emerging, unprogrammed situations and we may have to change our strategy. Being aware of and responsive to the actions of others help us through those uncertain moments.

xviii) *Positive thinking* – Footballers believe they can win every time. The moment they consider defeat is the moment they are defeated. They have to believe in themselves and their ability to conquer the opposition, thus satisfying their fans and protecting their status. Every change begins in the mind. Your thoughts lead to your actions and consistent actions become habits. If you don't develop a habit of believing in yourself, it will be difficult to conquer your mountains, indeed your molehills will start to resemble mountains. Once you are realistic in your aspirations there is no reason for you to doubt yourself; just put in the preparation, engage in positive affirmations and consider that if it doesn't work out, *this too shall pass.*

xix) *Perseverance* – Footballers have to keep going. There is no doubt that they get tired after 90 minutes of consistent running, however they block out the pain as far as is possible, keeping at the forefront of their minds the goal they are pursuing. The game may go into an extra time and they must have the heart to run for an additional 30 minutes plus any further minutes that may be added. Many of us get tired quickly, we have very little staying power and when the going gets rough we retire our projects and move on to something else. "*Rolling stones gather no moss.*" The next project will not necessarily be easier and we may find that *the grass is not greener on the other side*. Stick with it - take your project to completion.

xx) *Instinct* – Irrespective of the level of coaching and instructions given to players, when they are on the field they are masters of their own destiny. They have to weigh the consequences of their actions against the risk of a goal being scored by the opposition. At that moment intellect is good but instinct is supreme. We too have to be in tune with our intuition and know when to take impromptu actions in the face of emerging situations. Our mentors have no access to our gut feelings; we have to be true to ourselves and recognise that instinct is an innate quality that enhances our decision-making.

xxi) *Self-control* – From time to time footballers get into brawls on the field if they feel they have been treated unfairly, disrespected or if their egos have been bruised. However, for the most part they do exercise self-control. One could argue that their restraint is attributed to the power of the referee's yellow or red cards which have an adverse effect on their team. Self-control is a key factor in emotional intelligence - one which enables us to exercise tolerance, understanding, forgiveness and patience. If we allow others to make us angry and we lose control we give away our power. If we don't regulate our emotions we lose opportunities and close doors that could lead to good places; indeed we harm our chances to make progress. At the very least we have to be tolerant, respect diversity, obey the law and pay taxes. No one wants to live in a lawless society where our security is compromised because people disrespect authority, disobey rules and ignore responsibility.

xxii) *Respect* – Footballers must show respect for authority. They will tell you how much they wanted to be in the starting line-up for games but their managers had other ideas. They may be substituted on the pitch and they have no choice but to respect their manager's decisions. Respect for self and others are key ingredients in personal and professional growth. Movers and shakers do not like disrespectful people and will not go the extra mile to help even when it costs them nothing. The Jamaican proverb: *"Manners takes you through the world"* conveys this well.

xxiii) *Professionalism* – It must be very painful to lose a game, especially the ones that impact league tables or which are played on the international stage. Despite any disappointment or aversion, players shake the hands of their opponents and they often cheer them at the end. Even when they are suffering an embarrassing defeat they don't abandon the game. Whatever we do we should ensure that we adopt a professional approach. It is tantamount to integrity and these are the factors that make us look good and add value to our repertoire. In our life's work we must engage what I call E-principles – *efficiency, effectiveness, ethics, environment and economy*. We could also add *excitement, energy, and excellence*. We must endeavor to undertake our responsibilities with integrity, ensuring that we do not waste resources and are considerate of the environment which we all share.

xxiv) *Self-Discipline* – Despite what people may think, footballers are generally highly self-disciplined. Successful footballers have to be careful about what they consume, they have to refrain from certain vices and they have to ensure that they have sufficient rest in order to keep themselves ready for the start. We too must maintain self-discipline if we are to achieve our goals. We know what we have to do but often fail to do it or we procrastinate and make excuses. There is no sense in putting off your life; this is the moment we have and we must ensure we do not waste it, for tomorrow is not promised.

xxv) *Courage* – Watching a penalty shootout is a very tense moment even for those who do not play the game. Imagine therefore the fear that the penalty taker must feel, aware of the responsibility on his shoulders. If left unmanaged fear stifles creativity stopping us from taking risks that could propel us forward and curtailing our drive. It is a natural phenomenon that we all experience but we have to develop strategies to control it. There is always the temptation to avoid uncomfortable situations but we do not grow in comfort. It is only when we confront our fear that we truly understand what it takes to overcome. *Feel the fear and do it anyway* (Susan Jeffers).

xxvi) *High earning* – Footballers earn significant incomes. They find their purpose, play with passion and earn well from their chosen career. They do not waste time in roles that do not pay well and if they are not playing well, they are replaced. We too must find worthwhile opportunities and ensure we are making good use of our time and earning our worth. While it is fine to be in entry level jobs for a while, the onus is on us to grow professionally so that we can add value that positions us to meet our needs and be a blessing to others in due season.

xxvii) *Work hard, play hard* – We have already established that footballers work hard. They play hard too. It is not unusual to see photographs of them in the press enjoying themselves in some faraway place with their mates or loved ones. In our aspiration to acquire the finer things in life we often forget to have fun. We end up taking work home, working overtime, just to make a few extra bucks to *save for a rainy day*. Unfortunately by the time we get around to enjoying our savings many of us find ourselves alone, ill or may even be dead. Remember, a*ll work and no play makes Jack a dull boy.*

xxviii) *Patience* – There are often debates about whether a manager should be fired after an unsuccessful period or if such a manager should be allowed to complete his intended contractual tenure. Often it takes a while for success to be achieved. The board, players and fans alike often have to exercise patience and allow the team to gel under the manager's leadership. *Patience is a virtue*; too often we give up early because we don't immediately see the results we are hoping for. When the answers are not forthcoming we have to learn to be still. Because we live in a rapidly changing and demanding society, we feel we have to keep up the pace and thus we venture into areas prematurely, with the aim of making a headway. While this is understandable, there is a time for everything and though you may not agree with nature's timing, you will find that many a step poorly taken might have yielded better results if you had the patience to wait. There is a Jamaican saying - *the darkest part of the night is just before dawn.* There will be difficult moments but with patience and hard work we will *see the light at the end of the tunnel.*

xxix) *Gratitude* – Many footballers, indeed many sportsmen will tell you that one of their greatest joys was the fact that they were able to purchase property for their parents. Many will have assisted their friends and family to set up business, settle debts or purchase expensive items. We too must not forget our roots; we must reach out to those who helped us in our formative years and those who may have struggled with us before we achieved success. There is a famous quote that says: *be careful how you treat people on your way up because you might meet them again on your way down*. One way to express gratitude is to avoid the urge to take things for granted. Develop a habit of gratitude – be grateful for the sun, rain and moon if you can't find anything else to be grateful for. Why? Because they make the plants grow and plants are a primary source of food, medicine and other vital resources. There is so much to be grateful for; take a moment and give thanks.

xxx) *Generosity* – From time to time we hear of sportsmen who have donated money and resources to individuals. It could be as simple as purchasing drinks for everyone at a venue or leaving a handsome tip at a restaurant. They generally do not count their pennies; they focus instead on bringing in the pounds. In life we too must be generous with our resources. It doesn't have to be financial help – giving of our time, effort, know-how, physical resources, among others is just as good. For those of us who do business we must ensure that we negotiate win/win contracts so that all parties feel valued. There is no need to attach receiving to our giving; indeed giving is the seed for receiving.

xxxi) *Philanthropy* – Right across the world there are projects that are set up and/or funded by sportsmen. Altruism goes beyond one's immediate social group and extends out to humanity, perhaps building a school, funding a charity, purchasing equipment for a hospital, developing a sport facility within a community. Human beings must seek to leave a legacy, however small, not only to our family but to the world. We are duty-bound to support our own children but how many of us help other people's children? We may not be able to help everyone but surely we can each help someone.

xxxii) *Hard work brings true joy* – As we watch the various teams go for glory, one cannot help but cheer, irrespective of our allegiance. When you listen to their stories and see how far they've come you recognise how deserving of their places they are. They believe in themselves, work well as a team, remain calm under pressure, exercise patience, perseverance, professionalism and discipline; they conquer their fear, plan their strategy and execute their plans. At the end of the tournament they can be proud of representing their countries, regardless of the outcome.

Every aspect of our life is packed with lessons to be learnt and shared. These are some that the beautiful game of football can teach us. Let us explore and implement these factors in our lives and endeavour to build a legacy so that future generations can stand on our shoulders. *The heights by great men reached and kept were not attained by sudden flight, but they, while their companions slept, were toiling upward in the night* (Henry Wadsworth Longfellow).

ABOUT THE AUTHOR

Andrea Campbell, MBA, MA (Hons)
Social Entrepreneur, Author, Inventor & Linguist
https://andreacampbell.co.uk
https://uk.linkedin.com/in/andreacampbell6806
https://www.facebook.com/andrea.campbell.336717
https://twitter.com/camptys

CHAPTER 4

TOMORROW IS NOT PROMISED

By Agnes George

Many years ago, on a cool summers afternoon I met an amazing, handsome man; we were introduced by my best friend at a birthday party. Initially I did not like him but, his persistence and perseverance won, and eventually he became my husband. I then realized that when you find the one, you know, it is effortless. We had a wonderful life together, the type of husband every woman would dream of.

We did everything together, we were inseparable. We both enjoyed music and entertaining, he was very thoughtful, never forgetting a birthday or an anniversary.

Initially, he was a terrible cook, but he was willing to learn. I am a great cook myself, having learned my skills from an amazing chef and restaurateur at a French cookery course in Brittany, France. I taught my husband everything I knew about cooking generally and for entertaining at special occasions, as we did regularly entertain friends at home. But one afternoon whilst seated at a dinner table enjoying an amazing meal with close friends everything changed. It would alter my life forever.

My husband turned to me and said I am not feeling well. I have this excruciating headache; which has raised concern, he looked quite pale. He had never complained of headache before, which clearly demonstrated the severity of pain he was experiencing. He was taken to the Accident & Emergency Department by Ambulance where he was diagnosed of having sustained a massive brain haemorrhage, requiring immediate surgery to save his life. He was transferred to a specialist hospital, surgery was eventful, followed by a remarkable recovery; but three months later the symptoms re-occurred. He had to be hospitalized for a second time as an emergency because of secondary complications, which required further investigations prior to his surgery to relieve pressure on the brain, which was causing the headaches.

He was also diagnosed with type 2 diabetes; and during surgery sustained paralysis of his left side, which left him devastated. Being a very independent and proud individual who loved sports, enjoyed the outdoors and socialising, he did not cope well with the adjustments and diagnosis. He lost his independence, was wheelchair bound, needing help and assistance with his daily needs at a young age; he found it very difficult adjusting.

Whilst receiving rehabilitation treatment three days before his birthday he wanted to have a private birthday celebration with champagne between both of us and requested no visitors on that day. He had his wish for his private party.

He looked extremely well-dressed in his casual clothes. Before toasting, I asked him what shall we toast to? He looked at me with that cheeky smile, took my hand, looked straight into my eyes and said, "now raise your glass. A toast to 'just being here'". I thought it was odd, but dismissed it, and planned to visit him in the morning, but I overslept, was awakened by the telephone, it was the hospital ringing to say that my husband had passed.

That was the worst moment of my life; feeling shocked I could not breath, my heart was pounding as if it was going to jump out of my chest. For me tomorrow never comes, the way he hugged and held me so tightly when leaving him for the last time I failed to read the signals.

The news of his passing shook my world. The early days friends and relatives even strangers were really supportive; but then comes the realization that these people have to return to their various lives. I felt a feeling of over-whelming despair, got on an aeroplane to travel a twelve hours flight to be with my mother and best friend, the most hilarious, amazing phenomenal woman I know.

How I found my passion for International Speaking and Entrepreneurship.

This is how I found my passion. I realized that what had happened to me was preparing me for better things and it made me stronger, to become the woman that I am becoming. I trained as a certified World Class Speaker, became an Entrepreneur and the founder of the Health & Mental Well-Being Company working for myself. I provide a service to many people, speaking and managing my own events, offering one to one coaching, mentoring, doing workshops, and speaking Internationally at events, conferences, and secondary schools, from medical students and to junior doctors at the University of the West Indies. That was my giving back to my country. I have been interviewed by the Governor General His Excellency Sir Rodney Williams and Lady Sandra Williams at His Excellency's Residence in Antigua & Barbuda; and have also been interviewed by The Observer Radio presenter at the Antigua Observer Radio Station on the Topic of "The Prevention of Type 2 Diabetes" whilst visiting the country as a speaker on International Women's Day.

My mission is to reach millions of people globally speaking at events, and I see Powerhouse Global Platform as a member on the right platform to enable me to reach a bigger niche of millions of people from a diverse ethnicity.

The importance of forming the company is to provide a healthy lifestyle and coaching service to everyone who is at risk of type 2 diabetes, starting from the very young children to the older people.

Our children are the future generation, through education we can change their mindset in adapting to healthier habits and encourage them to make healthier lifestyle choices, with a view of sustaining a healthy generation for the future globally.

As an entrepreneur I can make a global impact speaking, mentoring and coaching individuals in the prevention of type 2 diabetes. Preventing type 2 diabetes can save millions of lives. Ninety percent of people with diabetes have type 2 which comes on slowly, over the age of forty years. The signs may be obvious, or there may be no signs. According to current research the same number of people affected by type 2 diabetes is the same as the amount of people who have the disease and do not know that they have it. Because many people do not experience any symptoms.

It may be up to ten years to find out you have diabetes type 2, therefore it is very important to know your risk factors, and to take action. You are six times more likely to get type 2 diabetes, if you have a parent, or a sibling with diabetes.

Ethnicity and Race plays a big part in developing type 2 diabetes.

Here are some tips and advice on the prevention of type 2 diabetes which can help you to reduce your risks and manage changes to your lifestyle choices which many people struggle with:

The most common risk factors include, increase in weight, clinically (obese) abnormal blood pressure, cholesterol and triglyceride which is increase in your blood circulation; by changing one's habits of a lifetime is not easy, but it is worth the effort.

This is why it is believed that big co-operation people these days appoint a Coach to help them with their nutrition.

Working with many clients who struggle with diabetes, I feel passionate in helping those individuals in reaching their goals in prevention of the disease.

Type 2 diabetes is preventable and reversible, but there is no cure for the diabetes, once you have been diagnosed with the disease, you have the disease for life. If it is not managed properly, it is a chronic condition which can lead to very serious complications. Sometimes people think it is expensive to invest in health, people pay much more in medicine; your health is your wealth, but if you do not have good health, the question is, what else is there?

As an entrepreneur I work in my business with serious clients who wantsto maintain good health. These are some tips and advice to help individuals. Most important is that you check your risk factor of developing diabetes, by taking the diabetes life risk assessment test, and learn more about your risk of developing type 2 diabetes. A score of twelve plus indicates that you are at high risk and maybe eligible to my program. This helps you to reduce your risk of type 2 diabetes, kidney disease, leading to kidney failure, diabetes retinopathy, a long-term complication of the disease which can damage the eyes leading to blindness, other complications, cardo-vascular disease and heart attacks.

It is very important in terms of weight management, because excess belly fat, especially if stored around the abdomen, can lead to type 2 diabetes.

Exercising regularly, by doing regularly moderate physical activity on a daily basis, helps manage your weight, reduce your blood glucose levels, may also improve your blood pressure and cholesterol. It is recommended walking 10,000 steps daily.

Eating a well-balanced diet is recommended, a healthy diet reduces the fat in your diet, especially saturated and trans fats. It is advisable to eat more fruits, vegetables and high fibre foods, and cut down on salt. It is recommended to limit take away and processed foods, convenience meals are especially high in salt, fat and kilojoules. It is better to cook for yourself using fresh ingredients whenever possible. It is suggested that by limiting your alcohol intake. Too much alcohol can lead to weight gain and may increase your blood pressure and triglyceide levels. Men should have no more than two standard drinks per day and women should have no more than one standard drink daily.

It is advisable to quit smoking; help can be obtained by attending the smoking cessation classes provided by the National Health Service (NHS), as smokers are twice as likely to develop diabetes as non-smokers.

If you were to be asked, how much sugar have you consumed today what will you say? Try to keep to the recommended standard. Every eight seconds somewhere in the world someone dies as a consequence of diabetes. So the next time you are tempted to over indulge in the foods that you love, remember sugar is not your friend, and you are eating yourself into a disease state for which there is no cure. The life expectancy of someone with diabetes is about six years less than someone without the disease.

Quote: "Health is the money we never have a true value of, only to realise its true value until you lose it". K. Josling.

This is what happens when you do not take action - life stops between your fingers.

ABOUT THE AUTHOR

Agnes George is a Transformational Coach, NLP Practitioner, Health Strategist, and an International Inspirational Speaker on the prevention of Type 2 Diabetes. Born and raised in the Caribbean, she became a teacher, but had to follow her passion of nursing and midwifery so moved to the United Kingdom and has been living in London for more than 35 years as a Nurse and Midwifery Manager, bringing up her son. She now helps people to live a healthy lifestyle through Coaching and mentoring. Agnes has always been passionate in helping and supporting her clients to live a healthier and more fulfilling life through education, coaching and by making good healthy life choices. She believes that everyone has a right to be healthy and that everyone can achieve and maintain good health through health education and support from a coach; and that we can achieve anything with the right mindset by never allowing our past habits to influence our future health choices.

Agnes started as an Entrepreneur to help and educate individuals in Diabetes Awareness. Her passion is improving the health & Mental Well-Being of individuals; by enabling them to live a healthy lifestyle; founder of the Health & Mental Well-Being Company, an International Inspirational Speaker, Transformation Coach, Diabetes Health Strategist, a speaker on the subject, client coach, and she organises and speaks at her own event. Her main coaching clients are corporate / busy professionals >40 years, and teenagers, for which she gets successful coaching results, with good feedback from clients. She speaks Internationally on diabetes raising awareness to educate many people and to add value to people's lives and she has dedicated her life to the prevention of type 2 diabetes, which is something that is very close to her heart.

Agnes is a member of the Global Woman Club, the Professional Speaker's Association and International Women Connected and has successfully made a great impact in the lives of teenagers, young children, men and women globally through speaking, coaching and mentoring engagements, workshops, mentoring.

Her mission is to inspire, educate and transform lives, having personally witnessed the devastation that diabetes caused her and continues to cause friends, families, and clients that she has cared for. This is her 'why' - the reason why she is so passionate about the prevention of the disease because, this disease can be prevented, it is reversable if diagnosed within the first 10 years of being diagnosed. Diabetes is a chronic condition, once you have been diagnosed with the condition you have it for life. There is no cure for the disease, current research is ongoing.

Facebook: www.facebook.com/agnes.george332
Linkedin: linkedin.com/in/agnestgeorge/
Twitter : @Rodd99George

CHAPTER 5

THE JOURNEY

BY BOLATITO AYOOLA

LIFE THEY SAY IS A JOURNEY

Journey by literary definition means an act of travelling from one place to another. Another definition however says 'A long and often difficult process of personal change and development'. These two definitions of journey apply to me.

I was born and raised with a plastic spoon. My parents were teachers and in those days, teachers like other civil servants were not only poorly paid but were never paid on time, sometimes they could be owed up to six months salaries before being paid and sometimes they would have to go on strike for a couple of days or weeks before they could get paid and not even in full.

Apart from the financial challenges that my family faced, The Western Region of my country then used to transfer my dad who was a secondary school principal from one town to the other, that gave me and my siblings education instability. Ask me how many primary schools I attended, I can't say, I practically lost count. I ended up finishing my secondary school education at the age I was to be graduating from university.

Getting to higher institution was not easy for me and sustaining myself was a big challenge. And that is when my real journey started. It was a decision I made…. TO SUCCEED NO MATTER WHAT. A very hard decision considering what I have being through before securing admission into College of Education. How did I end up in College of Education? I wanted to go university straight after my Secondary School graduation but I could not pass the entry examination into the university. I had to go to College of Education to obtain NATIONAL CERTIFICATE IN EDUCATION {NCE} for three years. Thereafter, I proceeded to university to study Language Arts. For my first degree, I was awarded BA{EDU}Language Arts.

Growing up was a real journey for me. I grew up to be resilient, hardworking, focused, determinant, disciplined, consistent in the pursuit of my dreams and not giving up. Self-sufficiency was my watch word then. I watched my hard working mother who was also a primary school head teacher venturing into all sorts of investments to make ends meet. Despite the financial challenges we faced, my family was still envied, lots of people still fed on us, my parents still helped other families and sponsored other children in school. Sometimes I wonder how my parents were able to achieve all that. It actually did not take me long to realise you really do not have to be rich to make an impact on other people's lives. From the little that God blessed my parents with, they were able to impact other people's lives positively.

When I was in College, right from my first year to my final year, after paying my school fees, I had some money kept aside for business and because there was no proper awareness of banking system then, I invested the money in buying fairly used cloths to sell to my friends in school. I encouraged them to pay me in three instalments so that I would not spend the money recklessly. Apart from that, I learnt hairdressing, so I was able to make hair for a few of my friends at a very low charge. This I did to sustain myself in College.

Fast forwarding to life after College, because my mum was always into so many ventures to sustain the family, I decided to do the same. I took up a teaching job in a secondary school, started my degree and at the same time registered myself in a fashion school and was also doing petty trading with it. Why do I have to do all these? My parents taught us values of life, and one of them is to be self-sufficient in everything, especially in finance. I decided to equip myself financially before marriage so that I would not be a burden to my husband, but be equal in all things, although I was not sure if I would marry a rich, poor or average man. Financially, whoever would be my husband did not actually matter to me.

After, my graduation from University, I continued with my teaching job which I really enjoyed, finished my training at the fashion school, and because I was able to save some money, I opened my own FASHION HOUSE which I named then 'TITO TAILORS'. This I managed for a very long time together with my teaching job and other petty trading I was doing. A few years after my marriage, I had the opportunity to travel abroad for buying and selling business. So I became an International Business Woman.

The journey of my life between College, University, Graduation, Business and Marriage were very rough, so many obstacles, thorns on the road, rejections, disappointments, trials and struggles, failures, dangers, criticisms and moments of sorrow and wanting to give up, it was a long processing time for me but I chose not to give up.

Going back to my childhood days, I remembered there was a time we had no fancy cloths, no fancy jewellery, no fancy shoes, one pair of school shoes for a whole academic year and before the end of that year, there would be lots of holes in the shoes that would need patching up. We had to manage our school uniforms, but we were never hungry though we could go for days without meat or fish, all because my mum never gave up on making sure she fed not only her family but everyone around us, she could not stand seeing anyone hungry. Despite all this, we were not only happy, but satisfied and very hopeful. I tapped the energy of not giving up from my mother. She is 89 now, but by the time you have ten minutes conversations with her, she will be asking you about business and ideas on how to make money to bless other people and as old as she is, she believes she can still be useful financially to everyone around her. She spends her pension on widows and the needy. I grew up to know my mum as a blessing to other people, every money she made from her businesses even her salaries and pensions were never for her, but everyone. This is how I want to live. I want Kingdom wealth and that is why I refused to give up because I want to be blessing to everyone around me.

POVERTY MENTALITY

Poverty according to literary definition is a state or condition in which a person or community lacks the financial resources and essential for a minimum standard of living. Poverty can also be defined as not having enough money for basic needs such as food, drinking water, shelter, toiletries and so on. To me, Poverty can be very DANGEROUS if I refused to recognise that everything I have including my life is a gift and be GRATEFUL for what I have. I realised that I practically don't deserve anything. So I am always GRATEFUL to God for the life I have and having realised this, I chose another state of mind which is HAPPINESS.

Happiness replaced Poverty Mentality in my life having realized that my financial state is a training ground, I am in this world to learn and not compete with anyone.

I also considered STATUS SYMBOL to be arbitrary, I don't have to adopt other people's status symbol like a big stylish mansion, latest cars and wardrobes full of designer clothes, shoes, bags and jewelleries to be HAPPY.

CONTINUOUS LEARNING AND PERSONAL DEVELOPMENT gave me another strength to keep moving. I chose to read inspiring books, the stories of the people that struggled and eventually overcome poverty through their hard work and resiliency to inspire and encourage myself. I placed value on myself and this helped me to determine what I actually want in life.

What about AVAILABILITY? Doing all sorts of businesses and jobs at my early stage in life was to secure myself financially so that I could become a STAY AT HOME mother for my children. Raising them myself without committing them into any nannies' hands was my priority. We all want different things in life, but there was one thing I lacked when I was growing up as young teenage girl, my mom's attention. Yes, she was jack of all trade, a very busy and hard working woman but she took our growing up for granted. So many intimate things I would love to discuss with my mum and I couldn't because by the time she finished all the work for the whole day, she would be tired, bath and off to bed after family prayer session. This I didn't want my daughter to live with. I eventually started a business that would give me good income and at the same time be there for my children physically, emotionally, mentally, financially, socially and spiritually. Watching them growing over the years has given me so much joy that all the riches in the world can never give.

YOUR ASSOCIATION MATTERS!

I also chose to surround myself with the RIGHT PEOPLE, hanging around the people with negativity will not only make you lose focus but also make you live a miserable life. There is this saying that you are who you hang out with. I carefully chose my ASSOCIATION and COMPANY. I realised that being in the midst of the people with low interest in good life, who lack motivation and initiative, low intellect, those who can't think independently, those who rely on assistance from other people, those who lack life skills and those who have bad training and upbringing can jeopardise my well-being and destroy my DREAMS and DESIRES. This led me to set BOUNDARIES. I refused to do things because other are doing it, I know what I want for myself so I don't follow the crowd. I do what's best for me and my family.

Thinking and acting like a DIAMOND. An average poor person thinks poorly of the so called RICH and SUCCESSFUL. They always have an excuse for other people's success and wealth. They investigate how this and that becomes successful, wealthy or rich. If I don't want to be poor, I have to think and act like a DIAMOND. With this I grow to appreciate, honour and respect everyone, rich, poor or average. Everyone with his or her own potential. I go out every day, believing that I CAN SHINE like a DIAMOND so I walk, talk and smile like A DIAMOND ♦

ABOUT THE AUTHOR

Bolatito Ladapo Ayoola is a mother of 4 children who believes that being a single mother does not mean you cannot achieve your potential and live a quality life.

Once a teacher they say is forever a teacher. She used her teaching experience and education background to raise her four children single handed And today, she is a proud mother.

A Marketing Consultant, Event Coordinator, Photographer, Global Recruiter, Passionate Business Owner with Forever Living Products (The Aloe Vera Company) and an incredible Team Builder in over

16 countries including United Kingdom, Canada, United States Of America, United Arab Emirates and Nigeria.

Believing that everyone is unique in their own magnificent ways, helping other people to achieve their potentials and make their dreams come true is her passion. She wants everyone, men and women, become to financially independent and live a healthy life.

A business coach and mentor who loves mentoring teenagers and young adults to identify their God given career at the early stage in life and coaching business owners to build their businesses.

Every stage of life comes with its own challenge they say. At some point in my life, I had to choose between being in a corporate world of 9-5 work pursuing my career as a Marketing Executive or be a stay at home mum. I love my children and I was ready to make the sacrifice for them.

Becoming an entrepreneur, working from home and being self-employed was my best option as I wanted to be the one to wake them up in the morning; pray with them; give them morning kisses and hugs; make their breakfast; take them to school; hug and wave 👋 bye-bye to them at the school gate; get their lunch and dinner ready before picking them from school; help them with their homework; pray with them and see them to bed.

I wanted to be as close as possible to my children to understand their pains, emotions, excitements, hurts, moods and even 'crushes'. I wanted to be their mentor, teacher, best friend, confidant and partner.

I wanted to give them all the necessary support to grow and pass through every stage of their lives till they become young adults.

It was at this stage of my life that I started my journey with Forever Living Products. I loved my marketing career and what I was doing but needed to be there for my family.

Over the years, I have enjoyed watching my children grow and working for myself has been a great and exciting journey so far. I have the flexibility I could not get from corporate job. I am able to spend more time with my family at my own comfort with an exciting income package.

https://www.linkedin.com/in/bolatito-a-4240aa28
Twitter: https://www.twitter.com/bbdomains

CHAPTER 6

TOGETHER ON THE FAR SIDE OF EXHAUSTION

By Diane Curley

"Dare to lead", they told us… "it's our time", "lean in", "get a seat at the table", "climb the corporate ladder", "shatter the glass ceiling". And this is what else we heard: "don't speak at this meeting, know your place, it's not your place, it's not personal, don't be so emotional, be vulnerable, be authentic, be true to yourself, who do you think you are? Don't try…do, never let them see you sweat, don't cry, be strong, dress like this, not like that, I cannot believe you wore that, you wear your heart on your sleeve, you're weak, you're too tough, just compromise, just ask, the answers always no if you don't ask, NO - salary is not negotiable, I can't pay you more than I pay him/her, it's policy, be grateful, be quiet, behave, be more, be less, you want more? You have to work harder, longer, prove yourself, start at the bottom, work your way up, come in early, stay late, pay your dues, don't complain, fit in, stand out, you just don't fit in, lead by example, lead with confidence, lead with authority, be flexible, take it down a notch, don't be so assertive, don't be so sensitive, don't be soft, you're too easy, too difficult, too loud, too much, keep it simple, you're overthinking this, do a deep dive, now dive deeper, ask why, what's your why? That can't be why, that can't be right, watch your tone, do not overreact, do not react, be proactive, who told you that you could do that? Just do it, show some initiative, be ambitious, there she goes again, can't she just do what she is told? Follow orders, follow through, follow up, follow his lead, stay in line, stay in your lane, stay alert, stay sharp, stay ahead, go back where you belong, you don't belong here, she's not meeting expectations, she's not performing to standards, just be friendly, be likeable, you can't be friends with everyone, not everyone is going to like you, you're in charge?, you're not in charge here, who's in charge? Why is she in charge? Somebody needs to put her in her place. Honestly, who does she think she is?"

She is all of us. And she is exhausted. Exhausted from the fight, exhausted from having to wrestle with the lies she had been told to keep her down and hold her back. Somewhere along the way women were told we needed permission. Sadly it was true, historically (and even now for some women around the globe) we needed permission to vote, permission to work, permission to say no, permission to decide if or when to have children, permission to have our own bank account, permission to change our minds, permission to serve on a jury, permission to decide what is true and right for ourselves, permission to think, permission to wear pants, permission to enter into legal contracts, permission to hold elected office, permission to own property, permission to keep our earnings, permission to earn equal pay, permission to marry, permission to have a childhood, permission to live without any form of violence, permission to be free, permission to live our identity, permission to choose who we love, permission to protest, permission to speak, permission to drive, permission to attend school, permission to lead, permission to live.

We have lived these shared experiences, travelled these tough roads. Sometimes together, often alone, or perhaps at different times, but we have lived it. And something happens when we have lived a shared experience. Living the shared experience binds us together in unity; and as we are united in the shared experience, we are then united in our willingness to act and effect change for the benefit of the greater good. This often happens in times of crisis: war, famine, natural disaster, disease, oppression. Tough times. Tough roads. Its' been said that tough roads create tough people. Here is what I know to be true-tough people are resilient, brave, and everywhere. Fortunately, for all of us, brave women historically fought and still fight for our rights and to them we are eternally grateful. But what happened? Why are we still travelling along these tough roads? Why are we still crossing the same bridges? Why are we still wading through these muddy waters? What needs to change so that women who lead can lead equally in any and every aspect of life?

Us. We need to change. And we need to be the ones who lead the change. We need to lead a revolution. A daily revolution.

Let us begin by letting go…

> things change;
>
> seasons change;
>
> people change;
>
> let go and adventure on…
>
> be wild and free…
>
> it's time for a revolution.

Come together on the far side of exhaustion. As we rest for a moment with our feet in a shallow pond or standing at the bank of the riverside, we can throw our ideas in as if it were a stone and cause ripples, make an impact. Yet let us not stay there too long, content and complacent. Let us swim upstream together, not to just dip our toes in the ocean, but to make big, beautiful waves of change. We need each other to help navigate the way, as sunglasses help filter the glaring sun that would normally blind us on our journey. The hot sand and the broken shells on our path will not deter us, because we know the beauty that awaits in the soul-restoring ocean, full of life. The way towards equality may be difficult and uncomfortable, or risky and dangerous, even so - it is necessary. Necessary to keep going, necessary to advance, to tear up the rules that benefit a few and not all, to uproot the status quo.

Let us meet at the corner of injustice and inequity. Let us open our arms and reunited, let us accompany one another as we travel these tough roads. Mobilized by our connectedness let us join others along the way, side by side, hand in hand, heart to heart, knit together with love so as to never to be separated again on the march toward justice and equity for all.

A few roadblocks…

We need to challenge the narrative; we are not here for your entertainment.

We need to change the messaging; we are not defined by our looks, other's definition of success, social media, our titles, the sum of our highs and lows, our mistakes.

We need to reject the double standard and the hypocrisy; while in similar situations men might be perceived as assertive, women may be perceived as aggressive. Men might be perceived as protectors, women may be perceived as overbearing; men might be perceived as intelligent, women may be perceived as arrogant, men might be perceived as persuasive, women may be perceived as bossy - you get the idea.

We need to transform the terminology, for instance, the word minority. Used as a descriptor, the word minority deprives us of our legitimate existence and separates us, contributing to a significant adverse effect within society. Here is the definition of minority as noted in dictionary. com: *noun, plural* mi·nor·i·ties.

1. the smaller part or number; a number, part, or amount forming *less than half of the whole.*
2. a smaller party or group *opposed to a majority*, as in voting or other action.

3. a group in society *distinguished from, and less dominant than*, the more numerous majorities.
4. a racial, ethnic, religious, or social subdivision of a society that is *subordinate to the dominant group in political, financial, or social power* without regard to the size of these groups.
5. a member of such a group.

Synonyms for minority include "opposition", "the outvoted", "less than half", "the few", "the outnumbered", "splinter group". When used to describe us, these words have a negative connotation and are dehumanizing. Let us advocate for encompassing and positive terminology. We exist together, in community. Let our words reflect this relationship. We need to turn away from a them vs. us mindset. We need to shift our focus to all of us. We need to speak up. We need to be heard. We need to be visible. We need to listen. We need to learn from each other. We need to create a platform of inclusiveness. We need to become champions of each other.

The road less travelled…

Opportunities exist to be visible, to speak up, to be heard, to listen and to learn, to be inclusive, to be champions of each other; let us leverage those opportunities and where they do not exist, let us create them. One avenue is eWomenNetwork (www.eWomenetwork.com) a premier global business organization with over 500,000 members in chapters connected throughout the world, offering programs, networking events, coaching, podcasting, speaking engagements, conferences, etc.. eWomenNetwork is an inclusive community that has grown year after year for over 20 years and continues to be at the leading edge of business and economic growth for women. Another route is All Ladies League (www.aall.in) creating opportunities for women to connect beyond borders and through their World Economic Forums, where women are invited to be the voices for change, and the leaders of change. Forums are held throughout the world, creating unlimited opportunities for growth, connection, collaboration and community.

At the crossroad of inspiration and celebration, Celebrating Women LLC (www.CelebratingWomenUSA.com) creates a path for recognizing and celebrating women through events and interviews. All women from throughout the world are encouraged to join the free project. Participation is as easy as typing your answers to the interview questions into the online form, uploading your chosen photographs with your submission, and Celebrating Women does the rest! The completed interviews are visible on eight social media platforms, challenging the narrative and influencing social media's message, with plans to publish the unifying collection of women's inspirational stories in book format. Celebrating Women champions women from all walks of life, amplifying women's voices, while demonstrating that every woman is a role model.

Another path forward in just three steps:

1. **Mentorship.**
    There is significant value and opportunity in mentorship, i.e., the leader who brings you along. Mentoring does not necessarily need to be a formal arrangement. I loved sharing an office with a leader, Patrice Kelly, years ago as I got to see her role firsthand, how to put out all the "fires" that rose up before her, and what I could do to support her, even as she supported me. She created opportunities for growth. I went along with her to meetings I did not need to be at for decision making purposes, but purely as opportunities for my growth. My thoughts were respected. My time valued. We did not always agree, but we always talked things out and came to a win-win solution. I was intact and whole. I remember when I was offered a significant role outside of the company, she encouraged me to accept the position, knowing I had outgrown my role; I outgrew my role because of her leadership and mentoring.

    Another leader and mentor, Sandra Yancey, refers to mentors as "femtors" denoting the female presence, and engrained within her company's values are a culture of "give first, share always, lift as we climb". Patrice & Sandra are 2 examples of women leaders who have paved the way on tough roads and integrate meaningful leadership into their roles.

Meaningful leadership involves nourishment: cultivating, fostering, sustaining, providing, & cherishing the relationship. Meaningful leadership evolves in an environment of living with a mindset of peaceful abundance and not anxious scarcity. If you live in a mindset of abundance, you always have more to give and no one can take more than you have, because you always have enough. If you live in a mindset of scarcity it might lead you to act out of fear, greed, comparison, and agitation.

What we all want and need is also within each of us to provide: supportive leadership, trusting relationships, collaboratively working to support a purpose-filled mission, with time, attention, interaction, and resources that work to people's strengths, and engagement - so as each of us shine, the whole team shines and the impact of our collective work is positive. I strive to be that leader; guided support if the team struggles, task to each individual's strengths, step back with trust in their ability as we stabilize, allow enough time to go through the process safely, ensuring the tools and resources are available that are needed, praise for the effort, seeking win-win outcomes, expressing gratitude, leading with grace, listening to understand followed by a thoughtful & helpful response. I do not always meet the goal I strive for as a leader and there is one area in particular that I continue to work towards, which is to recognize where my response falls short of compassion and then apologize. An apology does not diminish leadership, it enhances your ability to lead. I completely advocate for a heartfelt apology as a way of communicating your respect for others and building a trusting relationship.

2. **Communication.** Let us explore communication in more detail…effective communication is thought to be one of the hallmarks of good leadership. Effective communication has been described as the 7 C's: clear, correct, concise, complete, concrete, coherent, & courteous. And yet communication continues to be a source of complications. There is a need for improvement and recognizing this need, let us consider adding conversation as an adjunct to our leadership strategy. Conversation is used to provide support, deliver information, advance well-being, and involves techniques such as active listening, silence, clarification, paraphrasing, reflection, restating, providing leads, acknowledgement, focusing, and summarizing. In contrast, techniques such as challenging, probing, changing the subject, defensiveness, false reassurances, judgements, rejection, minimization and stereotyping are barriers to ideas and relationships. Conversation considers factors such as culture, beliefs, perspectives and perceptions, includes the offering of self and time, and can be embraced throughout business and industry.

3. **Mutual Support.** Mutual support is another strategy that benefits individuals and teams and can be transferred throughout business and industry. I consider mutual support as a form of advocacy, for myself and for others. It is more of a "I've got you" and "we're all in this together" mindset than simply task assistance and constructive criticism. Statements such as "I'm concerned" or "I'm uncomfortable" offer respectful and transparent acknowledgement of a need for change or intervention. Advocacy for everyone's physical and emotional safety is front and center, rather than judgement and blame. Requesting support is encouraged and equally as important as offering support.

   (Bonus step) PDSA (an acronym for Plan, Do, Study, Act) is a strategy learned alongside a team of visionary leaders during my time at CMMI (Centers for Medicare & Medicaid Innovation) and incorporates a system of organizing, implementing, evaluating and communicating projects, plans, or ideas. It is especially helpful to use this strategy in short, frequent cycles to achieve the outcomes, rather than to prolong any one part of the cycle, which can stall the process and delay completion. During the process, communicate the plan briefly, implement the plan, evaluate in real time and modify the plan as needed. Collectively communicate changes to the plan, completion of the process, and incorporate discussion surrounding what worked well, what did not work well, and what to change for the next cycle of PDSA. Communication and Mutual Support are inherent in the PDSA cycles.

Lessons learned along the way...

All the clichés, (and the leadership books that followed),"Dare to lead, lean in, get a seat at the table, climb the corporate ladder, shatter the glass ceiling" are in and of themselves degrading statements to women which are then followed silently or not so silently by a litany of do's and don'ts, have not served us well. I have heard those statements, and the do's and don'ts throughout my career and it pains me to say I heard them from other women. Yes. That is right, other women told me those things and more. Things like, "give me a list of everything you've worked on since you started" (which led me in future roles to keep track of projects on a calendar along with results, lest I was ever again asked to prove my worth). I have also had women whom I have admired as leaders then attempt to sabotage my work reputation because they felt threatened by my abilities. This has led me to ask questions during the interview process surrounding the company culture and tone of leadership. I look for a culture that aligns with my values and a team approach rather than top-down leadership. As leadership is both the position and the functions of the position, the hope is that leader is able and willing to lead marked by beneficial contributions, sound stewardship and positive influence. I appreciate their many contributions and lessons learned along the way. I do wish, however, that more of the lessons were about how to lead well, as opposed to lessons on how not to lead. Yelling, degrading, excluding, gaslighting, bullying, sabotaging, ridiculing, & controlling behavior are the lessons on how not to lead, learned along my career path from more women than I care to remember. Some of us, myself included, have been warned not to shine so brightly as you might shine brighter than the leader and that will not end well. If you do try to dim your light, you can be sure it will be too bright no matter what. I have chosen to not dim my light ever again. Honestly, I carry a flaming torch and I wear my sparkly crown, and as has been said "fix another woman's crown without telling the world it was crooked."

About that torch…

Over a decade ago, I read an essay by an undisclosed author published in the magazine *Working Mother* and I have been sharing it (carrying the torch) ever since:

>*the other woman…*
>
>"at some point in her career, every woman has shared challenges
>
>with another woman
>
>down the hall
>
>up the street
>
>in a corner office
>
>three thousand miles away.
>
>at some point in her career, every woman has needed

to compete with another woman

to fight on behalf of another woman

to place her trust in another woman

to interview another woman.

at some point in her career, every woman has needed another woman

to trust with her children

to remind her of who she used to be

to be a role model without ever knowing it

to listen.

at some point in her career, every woman should tell her story.

not for her, but for another woman not so different from herself.

change begins with understanding.

understanding begins with conversation."

Do not be afraid of the challenges, the roadblocks, the competition, the failures, the darkness. Do not give up and do not stop fighting. Do not wait for the light at the end of the tunnel. Carry your torch, and as heavy a burden as it is, hold it high and light the way. Go ahead and light another woman's torch. Your torch will still be ablaze with flames even as the flames of her torch begin to glow & rise. It took nothing from you and yet it gave everything to her. Empowered, together, keep going and light up the world.

About that crown...

It is sparkly and it shines brightly! I am a child of God, and as the daughter of Jesus, my One True King, I inherited my crown. My identity is in Christ, and I rest safely in the Lord's embrace with that knowledge. Along with the crown come gifts of love, peace, mercy, grace, joy, and kindness- just to name a few. My faith is wrapped up within these gifts and the crown reminds me of who I am in the eyes of Jesus. Faith has restored my soul over and over, saved me from despair, saved me from the crushing death of my very soul. I am stronger in my weakness, kneeling at the foot of the cross. I lay down my burdens at the foot of the cross as well. I find it easier to "lay my burdens down" than to "give it up" to God. It is just semantics, but the words make a difference in my ability. My ability to love and serve as my faith calls me to is also strengthened by words, specifically-The Word, the Gospel. I am compelled by the power of the Holy Spirit to share the Gospel, the Truth, the Way and the Life and I share not necessarily in words, but by serving as the hands and feet of Jesus on earth; providing medical care around the world to victims of crisis: war, famine, natural disaster, disease, oppression. During tough times. Along tough roads. And I am made strong and whole and tough, so I can do the "work". And I can do all these things, through Christ. I pray often to God in the name of Jesus and by the power of the Holy Spirit for Christ's strength, for God to go with me, for God's hand to be upon me. I pray for hope and peace and mercy and joy to follow me wherever I go. I pray to serve well. I pray that when I serve in His name, people "know we are Christian by our love', feel the love of Christ, and choose to follow Christ. And at the end of the journey I pray I hear, "well-done, good and faithful servant".

I wrote this short poem (inspired by the song *My Story* by Michael Weaver and Jason Ingram), to illustrate my walk with Christ:

"If I told you my story

You would feel Hope and never let go

If I told you my story

You would feel Love and never be alone

If I told you my story

You would hear of Grace that is greater than my all my fears

Of Forgiveness freely given and Mercy shared

Of the Kindness of others that draws me near

If I told you my story, you would hear of Service born of Freedom that was won for me

You would hear me speak of a Life full of overcoming & becoming the woman I was meant to be."

This is my story; I encourage you to share yours.

Now about those clichés…

Instead of "dare to lead", let us consider leading as if it were the most natural thing in the world for women to do.

Instead of "it's our time", as if it were one singular moment in time, now or never, let us consider that every moment is the right time for women to lead.

Instead of "leaning in", let us consider reaching out to grasp the hand of another woman and go together in the right direction.

Instead of "getting a seat at the table", let us consider standing up for one another.

Instead of "climbing the corporate ladder", let us consider linking arms, moving forward and rising together.

Instead of "shattering the glass ceiling", let us consider that our opportunities are limitless.

The turning point…

(Credit to Happy Givers NPO Founder, Carlos A. Rodriguez)

Jesus Protected Women

Empowered Women

Honored Women Publicly,

Released the voice of Women

Confided in Women

Was Funded by Women

Celebrated Women by name

Learned from Women

Respected Women

And spoke of Women as

examples to follow.

Our Turn.

Final Steps...

So, who does she think she is? Worthy. She is worthy. *We* are worthy.

As we come together on the far side of exhaustion, here is my battle cry for our daily revolution: Lead. Reach out. Speak. Influence. Create. Share. Gather. Root for each other. Celebrate as we grow. Do not give up. Give first. Give Back. If you fall, stand again, this time stronger, stand for another. Rise. Lift others. Succeed. Celebrate some more. She is not your competition. She is your sister. Do it together. For one another. As one. And this time... stay together.

ABOUT THE AUTHOR

Diane Curley MSN, RN, CNOR, CHCQM, FABQAURP

She believes in the transformative power of real-world human connections.

Leading Long Island's chapter of eWomenNetwork, a premier women's business network, Diane creates an environment where women professionals & business owners come together to create experiences that spark engagement, enable change, and enrich lives – to move women and businesses forward & in the right direction.

As Managing Director, Diane facilitates business events designed to share talent, knowledge, resources, & proven success systems, develop business relationships & personal connections, build and grow businesses collaboratively, & initiate professional advancement.

A Registered Nurse by profession, Diane serves her community providing clinical education & supervision at St. Joseph Hospital in Bethpage.

Passionately supporting the mission of Lelt Foundation, a non-profit organization based in New York, as Medical Director, Diane established partnerships to improve the health of the population in two communities in Ethiopia through increased access to healthcare & humanitarian aid.

Committed to meeting critical needs of victims of war, poverty, famine, disease and natural disaster, Diane serves on an International Disaster Assistance Response Team and has served the people of the Bahamas, Liberia, Nigeria, Ethiopia, refugees from Syria, Pakistan & Afghanistan in Greece, refugees at the US southern border, and most recently in NYC Central Park field hospital for Covid19 response.

Challenging the narrative & influencing social media's message, as CEO/Founder of *Celebrating Women LLC*, Diane created a platform for recognizing & celebrating women as role models, publishing a unifying collection of interviews about women. She believes by sharing our stories, we inspire each other, remember who we are, encourage one another, heal a generation, save the next & celebrate...because every woman is a role model!

www.eWomenetwork.com

CHAPTER 7

LIFE WILL NEVER BE THE SAME

Caroline Emile

It's the 19th of April 2018; a Thursday.

I'm at ExCeL London, the renowned exhibition and international convention centre, surrounded by thirteen thousand people from sixty seven countries. It's been a rather long day indoors, but it's finally time for us to make our way out.

It's already dark when I step outside, with a pleasant spring evening breeze. I walk slowly, tightly sandwiched between fellow attendees, in what could have easily been a scene from 'Exodus'. Though we're mainly strangers to each other, there's a palpable sense of unity amongst us following the day we've just shared together. The vibe is electrifying, with sporadic waves of positive mantras and applause breaking out around me.

'Yes!'

'Yes!'

'Yes!'

'Yes!'

And then I smell it; the distinct smell of burning coal! This should conjure up pleasant images of a summery barbecue with my friends and family, right? But instead, I'm suddenly jolted out of my euphoric state and a sense of panic wells up from my abdomen and fully envelops me. I still can't see beyond the drove of people ahead of me, but the smell has alerted me that I'm now close enough to the fire.

I swallow hard, almost in disbelief at the predicament I find myself in. It feels like a bad dream that I just want to end, but it doesn't. I feel stuck. Yet, I continue moving forward on autopilot.

The burning smell intensifies. My heart beats faster and faster. I eventually feel the coolness of grass against my bare feet, signalling to me that I've almost arrived. And sure enough, the last few people in front of me quickly fade away, and right there before my eyes is the ember glow of a 500 degree Celsius firewalk!

My mind is now literally screaming at me to stop walking! What had earlier seemed like an exciting idea now looks highly foolish. I remind myself that I don't have to continue, that I have free choice and can just walk away - no one would even know.

But another part of me has stepped up to my internal microphone, and is giving me a cool and collected pep talk: "If you can get through chemotherapy, you can get through anything! And remember, there are no coincidences", with what feel like a wink at the end.

And without further ado, I begin applying the instructions I'd been given over the last few hours; I look straight ahead, internally affirm "cool moss, cool moss, cool moss" and with utmost determination, stomp my way with clenched fists across the bed of burning coals in five or six steps, never once looking down.

Voila! I had just successfully walked across the toughest road I'd encountered in my 42 years of life.

And I don't just literally mean Tony Robbins' famed firewalk at his "Unleash The Power Within" event. You see, what my inner voice had reminded me of when it mentioned that there are no coincidences was the major significance of the 19th of April for me.

When I'd booked the event almost six months earlier, I wasn't aware of its exact date, let alone that a firewalk was involved - I was simply giving myself something to look forward to in the upcoming year. What 'coincidentally' transpired was that I went to bed that evening completely elated, and excitedly looking forward to the infinite possibilities that I felt lay ahead of me as a result of my overcoming the limitations of my mind. I had achieved the seemingly impossible. This was the polar opposite of how I'd gone to bed an exact year to the day earlier, when I'd received a breast cancer diagnosis.

In the interim year since the 19th of April 2017, I had experienced a roller-coaster of emotions: shock that the lump that had randomly appeared on my left breast was cancerous; fear; impatience to finish treatment; hope; dread; faithfulness, indifference and back to more fear. I underwent six rounds of chemotherapy, breast and lymph node surgery, 20 sessions of radiotherapy and hormonal treatment (a daily pill to minimise my oestrogen levels as the type of cancer I had was oestrogen-sensitive). All this was interspersed with a plethora of scans, blood tests and injections to various parts of my body.

And though I had completed the hospital-based part of treatment almost three months before the event, I was still relatively fragile with limited energy, black nails (courtesy of chemo) and not much hair (the majority of it fell during chemo). But most of all, I felt quite lost.

You see, after the initial celebratory vibe of completing the recommended hospital treatments for Stage 2 breast cancer had worn off, I felt a vast void looming ahead of me. The structured life that I'd led since being diagnosed - even if it involved gruelling experiences like chemo and surgery - had ended, leaving me without a clear roadmap for the next part of my life. Whilst my aim was to beat cancer, I had enjoyed having a definitive plan with distinct treatment stages, each with their own timelines telling me what I needed to do and who I needed to be to reach my desired destination.

But having arrived at this destination, I didn't know what was meant to happen next! I suppose I was just meant to slot back into my old life before the diagnosis, right?

Only I simply couldn't!

Whilst I was no longer an 'active' cancer patient, I couldn't fully cut my ties with the disease as I was still on hormonal therapy and was expected to have regular check-ups to detect recurrence (most occur within the first five years after diagnosis). So I couldn't fully go back to my pre-cancer life, yet I wasn't sure where I was meant to go next or if I even had the energy to move forward. It was like having one foot in the past, and one in the future; simultaneously being pulled back to the life I knew before April 2017, and meanwhile being yanked forward to a brand new reality that I had no user guide for.

I was basically stuck in a metaphorical no man's land ... a waiting room, until I was able to break free towards one direction or the other.

And so crossing over that bed of fire on the first anniversary of my diagnosis was an uber- symbolic moment for me, heralding that I'd finally dared to cross over to a new beginning – and in grand style too! It didn't matter that what lay ahead was still unchartered territory; it was simply enough for me to take the plunge forward despite my on-going fears, exactly as I had just physically done on the firewalk.

The next morning, back inside ExCeL for the second day of the event, 'Life Will Never Be The Same' by Haddaway was blasting to commemorate the significance of our breaking through our mental and physical limitations to walk on fire the previous night. The song naturally resonated with everyone, but for me, it wasn't just the theme tune of a symbolic fresh start with a renewed mindset, but of a literally new life path.

As the caterpillar sheds its old self to transform into a butterfly that is able to soar to new heights, I intended to use my baptism by fire (in this case, a literal one too!) to help me become the person I was born to truly be. I knew that I hadn't yet achieved my full potential, though I had qualified almost three years earlier as a life coach (whilst working in marketing communications). But I was more or less waiting for the world to discover my skills to inspire and empower others.

Fast forward a little under two years, and I've become a TEDx and international speaker that has spoken on three continents (having never previously spoken on stage!), the co-author of multiple global best-selling books and winner of the *Powerhouse Global Awards – Inspirational Woman Of The Year 2019* and the *Women Economic Forum Award - Iconic Women Creating A Better World For all 2019*.

None of which were things I'd have dreamt of achieving prior to cancer. But I believe that each of us has a unique purpose or mission in life, and that everything that befalls us comes to help us fulfil this. I have always believed this, perhaps because of my Christian upbringing, and so I trusted that cancer came to help make me the person I was created to be, rather than to break me. And so instead of wallowing in self-pity and asking "Why is this happening to me?" with a poor-me attitude after being diagnosed, I was instead pondering from the outset what cancer had come to teach me; who was I being invited to become and what was I being invited to do?

Which is what led me to sharing my journey publicly, first by launching a blog the very next morning after diagnosis, and later, it was what enabled me to overcome my fear of public speaking so that I could impact far more people across the world than I ever could through just one-to-one coaching or online posts.

Throughout my transformation to becoming 'butterfly me', or the best version of myself, fear continued to give me a piece of its mind (or – to be more accurate – a piece of MY mind), offering practical nuggets of logic like 'you can't afford to enrol on this public speaking training' or 'you don't need to do this TEDx talk, it's too soon for you, you've only been speaking in public a few months', and plenty more.

But I learnt to ignore my mind at such moments and to instead tune in more with my *soul*. After all, if I'd listened to my mind after reading all the consent forms prior to starting my treatment or before stepping on to the firewalk, I'd have never done either! I had first-hand practical experiences to reassure me that taking leaps of faith based on the desires of the 'non-logical' part of me (aka my soul/heart) had yielded positive results, and so whenever I felt resistance brewing within me to what was an initially wildly exciting desire, the more I knew I had to actively drop back from my head to my heart.

You see I believe that we wouldn't innately desire anything unless it's part of our fulfilling our highest potential. Yet, as a society, we've become too mind-oriented. We calculate each and every step: how much will this cost? What will my return be? What will so and so think or not think of me if I do/don't do this? What if it doesn't work out? What if I fail? What if . . . you get the gist of it!

I was most certainly guilty of this before cancer. And this is probably why I had become stuck in my life. After all, caterpillars aren't unhappy creatures. In my case, I had a good life with a good job and a full social circle. But it had become apparent by the time I was 35 that there was something missing. I felt like I was living the same year over and over again, maybe just with a different job title or some new friends here and there. But the core essence was the same. I was happy but unfulfilled.

And that's exactly what a comfort zone is.

Yes, I had taken a step forward to train as a life coach, but I had paced down completing my training to a logically comfortable speed, and I never truly 'dreamed big' from there. It was only thanks to cancer that I somehow gave myself the permission to throw away the shackles of comfortable living, one decision at a time.

I don't want you to wait for an adversity to strike you before you too give yourself this permission. Start listening to your soul/heart NOW, and instead of letting your mind talk you out of pursuing your 'wild' and 'illogical' desires, use it instead to plan how to achieve these. You see, it's a sequential relationship that helps us create fulfilment in our life – be led by your soul then implement through your mind.

This is how you'll truly fly, butterfly – so go on and unleash your best self!

ABOUT THE AUTHOR

Caroline is on a mission to inspire and empower individuals on every continent to unleash the best – or butterfly - version of themselves, with a view to creating a happier and more conscious world.

She professionally trained as a coach at the Co-Active Training Institute in London after working for almost a decade in marketing communications across various industries in the UK and Middle East, yet became more dissatisfied at her core as she progressed in her career. A redundancy from her 'dream job' (which ultimately became highly toxic), was seized by Caroline as an opportunity to finally embrace her innate passion to support others to reconnect with their authentic selves, and she embarked on coach training.

A breast cancer diagnosis a few years later prompted Caroline to pursue her passion more zealously. Having experienced first-hand the detrimental effects of an unbalanced 9 - 5 lifestyle, she overcame her introverted nature to become a speaker (including TEDx) to ensure that her message to live purposefully reached more corporate careerists across the world.

Egyptian-born Caroline is a global citizen who currently lives in London. She is co-author of 'Voices Of Hope' and 'Joy – Recipes For Abundance', and winner of the Powerhouse Global Award of Inspirational Woman Of The Year 2019 as well as the Women Economic Forum Award of Iconic Women Creating A Better World For all 2019.

www.butterflyme.co.uk

CHAPTER 8

STRENGTH AND WISDOM FROM LIFE EXPERIENCE

By Elizabeth Lucas-Afolalu

"Thinking right will enable you to build meaningful relationships, earn more wealth and be a fulfilled and successful happy person"
Elizabeth Lucas-Afolalu

Do you want to know the secret of overcoming any situation, enjoy freedom and be happy and How did we deal with other people's opinions, comparison, criticism and judgmental?

Many more questions to answer in this exciting and interesting chapter to read, learn and re-adjust, re-think again and re-invent your life. Everyone has suffered some sort of emotional hurt through the words or actions of another and experiencing this hurt is completely natural, but sometimes the hurt lasts longer than it needs to. This makes it harder to be happy and if we can't let go and move on, it can ruin our relationships. Someone that can never forgive is someone destined to be alone. In every challenge of life there are always storms and there are ways to come out of those storms, situations are not permanent. There is always movement however, storms and adversity force you to change and become stronger, every disappointment is a blessing, if the situation didn't kill you, it will make you stronger and if there is life, I still hope for the future.

Many people continue to carry their negative past experiences with them in the journey of life, and have lived lives marked with negativity and mediocrity. A life that is full of "I CAN'T," while afraid to step out of their comfort zone and out of poor self-confidence, low self-esteem, blaming others and complaining has been affecting several personal and professional lives today. The most successful and the happiest people in the world always work to improve themselves, to be better than they were yesterday, and it is this constant work on personal growth that brings them closer to their life goals every day. Nothing will change unless you change; nothing will get better unless you get better. If you want change, then you make that change. The body has its limitations, but the mind is not limited. The attitude and lifestyle of constant personal discovery and growth requires a specific mind-set that wants to learn and work on personal development, and will awaken in you the drive to discover more and to do more. This chapter will help you to acquire this mind-set with ease, and in the most natural way possible. When you renew your mind-set, then your life can be transformed and free, and you can be happy. For so many years, the statement of "YOU CAN'T" followed me everywhere. I heard it from family, friends, relatives, co-workers, colleagues, teachers, lecturers, managers, and trainers. However, God the Creator, who created ME, has proven them wrong! YES YOU CAN... it is not easy, but it is POSSIBLE. Start by believing God and believe in yourself. Based on what people have said to us, or said into our lives, we say to ourselves, "I have no talent;" "I'm not creative;" "I can't do it;" "I'm too old;" "I'm too young;" "I am not educated" I cannot speak in public, I cannot become", I can't achieve it", "I'm too weak", "I'm too dull", "I'm too tired;" "I'm too busy;" "People won't let me;" "I'm afraid;" "People don't believe in me;" "People won't listen to me", etc.

> *"Sometimes the people you love the most turn out to be the people you can trust the least"*
> *Trent Shelton*

People have got used to hiding from their emotions and to letting them govern their lives uncontrollably, which leads to many unresolved conflicts, inner and with others, to sending mixed messages to the people around them and to numerous lingering issues waiting to be resolved (which rarely happens. Because of this, the person who is in touch with their emotions, who knows how to control and understand them, and who is able to detach themselves from their feelings is often viewed as stable, professional and reliable partner, in business or in private life. And they really are, because they don't allow emotions to rule their lives. Challenges and adversity will only make you stronger even though you may feel broken and bruised now, you will recover from this ordeal and become more resilient person. When we get injured, the scar tissue that develops to mend our damaged skin is stronger than you could ever imagine. It's the same for your heart and soul: trust in their ability to heal, too. In keeping with this.

This chapter is about inspiring and motivating readers to do something, to renew their mind-set and start believing that they can do something, they can become and they can achieve. This gives you useful wisdom of how to, and important steps to take to climb the ladder of success. It's also open the way for you to be able to research for more wisdom and information, to seek professional advice and counselling. I am using this space to challenge and help you and others to come out of your comfort zone, keep challenging that you are not alone in your situations and that some people has turned their past and present experiences, situations, fears and circumstances into greatness. Nothing should stop anyone to become great or do something exceptional. No one is perfect and practice makes someone better if they try something new and reposition themselves for change.

Let me share with you a little bit of my story, I was born in London and then at the age of three, my dad took me to Nigeria to live with my relatives and to go to school however, the experience of being without my parent for several years before they returned from UK was traumatic. My life experience was full of shame, neglected, abandoned, rejected, isolated and on top of this, I was physically, sexually and verbally abused constantly by strangers, yes you heard me, I repeat strangers and by close family, relatives and friends. And while growing up, I was used and dumped in the name of love, tricked, maltreated and cheated and at a certain point, homeless, helpless and hopeless, I lost my identity, my position and birth-right was not celebrated in the family and I had no voice. All the negative words said to me and upon my life followed me for years that I also believed it and said it to myself for years, I became low self-esteemed, lacked boldness, lacked confidence and eventually believed it myself that I am nobody as they've said. I was afraid to do anything, to stand in front of people, to lead or to speak out in public and keep everything to myself and for that anyone that talked me down, use me and abuse me and took advantage of me lonely in the crowd and crying in the wilderness. On top of this, I was physically, sexually and verbally abused and this had resulted in me having very low esteem, lack confidence, afraid of being rejected or of speaking out, afraid to lead or of sharing my success. I was full of anger and frustrated, in self- denial, made a suicide attempt, always going behind the scene and pleasing people and going out of my way to help others, but neglecting myself and my purpose in life. I struggled to love and receive love and that was what I was afraid of before I got married.

I wanted to stay single to focus on my life and carry on improving myself and become successful in business and did that work? Oh no, I become committed in the name of love and entered into relationship with all this emotional trauma. On top of this, I settled with a traditional man that had a fixed mind-set of having a wife that will just be a housewife, illiterate and mother of his children to care for and instead of it getting better, it got worse. Marrying a man with another emotional trauma, we both went through everything you can think of, every storm, every crisis, both of us raising children without a sense of belonging, with no one to support me in this crisis. In addition, I felt controlled, criticised, abused and isolated, I was depressed, suicidal, sick and hated myself. I could not receive love and compliments but was always going out of my way to support and inspire others and working hard to sustain the family, believing that things will be better later. I became defensive, a perfectionist, assumption, afraid to speak in public, listening aggressively and not with my heart, controlling and negative. I belong to a denomination where my pastor was constantly teaching and dealing with all these issues and gradually, I outgrew those issues but not enough. I studied everything in the bible on love, kindness, patience, endurance and prayer, getting better understanding but still, it wasn't not enough, I sought for wisdom and having patience, I stayed, found solutions and dealt with the situation and overcame. Today we are still standing as couple and truly with love we can do anything – yes, we can. It takes two to mingle, I've turned the situation around, I have grown to become better, stronger and extraordinary woman to bounce back and support the man I love and to understand that every situation was for a reason. It was a platform for experiment and experience and I've turned the negativity to positivity, and no one is perfect but, if we are willing, we can get better, if you don't seek help you can't get any. If you don't ask you cannot receive, keeping silent and suffering in solution is not the best way and the situation can become worse if you don't cry out for help. It is also not about you alone but anyone you love, however your life is the priority. When you can develop yourself, other things can be taken care of, you cannot change others, but you can change yourself to attract and impact others and you need to make decisions for your life. With love, prayers, better understanding and patience, I've turned the situation around. I have grown to become better, strong and an extraordinary woman and to understand that every situation was for a reason, was a platform for experiment and a training ground. I've turned the negative situation to positive and became happy to love myself and others and to forgive myself and others, and be kind and continue the journey of life.

> *"The quality of a man is the state of his mind*
> *and future, you will only attract*
> *What you believe and think about"*
> *Elizabeth Lucas-Afolalu*

Another story about Janet and Jude concludes the story above: Janet got married to Jude and had wonderful children but her aspirations to get better were overturned, which was another stage of life living with a husband who believed Janet should just work hard for the family. Jude was insecure, with low-esteem and very controlling man who has no plan for himself, for the future or for the children. Janet continues to work hard and became the breadwinner for many years while the man was doing his own thing, wasting money and wasting time. Jude had the opportunity to stay permanently and work in a foreign country, he exploited every opportunity. He went from high school to university for six years, he choose not to look for a job while studying, he used excuses not to stay home to support the children, while his wife was working hard to feed the family. To make matters worse, he borrowed money from financial institutions, and unknown to his wife, he had loans from several banks and collected credit cards that he was unable to pay back. Even though he settled for a low paid job after his transitional education, he expected Janet to continue working hard to take care of him and the children and yet still he never treated her well.

However, Janet worked hard by working as an employee and also running part time small businesses and bought the family two properties, one on her name and the other one they lived in on both Jade and Janet's name. However, due to Jade's mismanagement of finance, Janet was forced to sell her own property in order to secure the house they lived in to protect her, the children and her husband from becoming homeless. Janet lived a life controlled by her husband, frustrated and isolated. She worked hard to see that the children lived in a good environment and attended very good school. Her commitment with her household affected her work, and several times she resigned from good jobs. Every move for Janet to progress to a better job or running a business has always been a threat to her husband who felt insecure. He would even try to find ways to stop her as doesn't want her to rise up above him in career, spiritually and in business. He consistently talked her down and always discouraged and criticize Janet. Jude has a way to control Janet, he will give Janet many reason why she should not associate herself with friends, relatives, he distracted and disturbed Janet, not to get involved in any activities, he was in full control of her movements as Janet is not driving and if she does he will still demand for her full attention at home.

One time, Jude told Janet not to seek a certain employment and not to have certain person as a mentor; he also demanded that only him if at all could see anybody he likes. He advises the departmental leader not to promote Janet, because he believed Janet cannot do anything and cannot speak nor lead anyone. He only wanted her to support him and his belief is to have a full housewife who will also go out and work hard to feed him and the children. But still Janet still aspiring to progress by learning how to manage the family, manage the finances and time and home and silently developing herself. Janet married a man full of himself, who deceived her and pretend to be nice, who uses emotional blackmail to control her, who is totally confused and will not admit he has problem, who is selfish and self-centred. This man will be happy if Janet only focus on him, do everything for him and no one else and Janet worked tirelessly to support the children's upkeep and schools up to university. Jude had no regard for anyone, has no mentor, has no elders to talk to him and has no friend to report him, he fooled himself and deceived himself and pretends to the whole world that he is the nice guy. He doesn't value the diamond in his domain nor appreciate the gifts and talents that Janet has. He doesn't believe in Janet and doesn't celebrate her. He very quickly criticises and condemned her, always looking for downfall and mistakes of his wife. He denied his wife and children that nobody including his care to know them. He enjoyed their presence only when the family isolate themselves in their room, and monitored their movements with his phone whenever they are out. However, Janet is determined to stay and deal with the situation in her own way. Janet stood by Jude in all this crisis and covered his shame and still cultivated the habit of being developing and improving herself, supporting the children and to be happy, always smiling and dreaming. One day herself and Jude will understand and love one another better, she believed with God's help, their relationship will be a testimony together with her relationship with parent, siblings and friends. She is determined to seek a solution to turn her situation around and become better.

What happen behind the scene?

During this moment Janet then focused on developing herself while she seeks solutions and practice what she learnt. She never gives up, quits nor end the relationship but use her energy to support others and inspire them daily, she turns her vulnerability to possibilities, her challenges to training ground and weakness to draw strength. She became successful in employment from low key job to higher position, became creative entrepreneur and writer, eventually became an award-winning author and international inspirational speaker. Her passion is to support and inspire other women and youths who may find themselves in this same situation or similar and she is ready to go out there to motivate, mentor and support millions of people. She aims to impact people's lives and her agenda on earth is to create an opportunity to reach out to next generations and encourage and prepare their mind-set and emotions to have a good relationship they deserve. Janet's belief is that if she can, everyone can also, and she will make every relationship and family in her life work - including her relationship with parent, relatives, friends and sibling, and also to be an inspiration to others. Every situation will make you stronger even if it feels difficult as it might just become a great opportunity for you to succeed. Janet keeps trusting and believing that one day, the table will turn around and both Janet and Jude will live fulfilling and happy lives and will be a channel of blessings to others. So, Janet keeps exercising patience and praying and aspiring to greatness by seeking help, reading books, attending seminars, and conferences, and listening to tapes to develop herself, and to continue inspiring and supporting others.

There is always glory behind every story - Today Janet has developed a good relationship with everyone and easily let go and forgive quickly. Janet has good working relationships with people everywhere she worked in various sectors and industries, she has worked through from lowest menial job of cleaning and healthcare assistant up to senior position of secretary and personal assistant to Directors, Manager and Chief Judges and various government departments. She has worked across different industries i.e. Government, Judiciary, NHS and Health care and Examination bodies. Janet has developed herself as a businesswoman to run markets, planted various stores and shops across United Kingdom including online and was successful.

Then she had a stroke, together with other health issues, however during recovery, she did not let that limit nor stop her journey of success, She educated herself to degree level in Business and Management in one of the top universities, University of Northampton in United Kingdom. She became the CEO and Director of businesses, Marketing Executive and Sale leader of companies. She is an evangelist, inspirational and motivational speaker, writer, mentoring Youths, Women, Relationship and Families, the author of 'Yes You Can' and UK Chief Editor Bureau for American Magazine - Okunsgroup Magazine, Secretary of the year and School Parent Governor in United Kingdom. Janet endured, developed herself and loves the same man she married. Janet became a prayer warrior and intercessor; she learnt lots from her experiences, from others and other products on relationship. She continues to persevere and is determined to let this relationship with everyone work through her personal relationship with kindness, love, forgiveness, caring and passions to support other women, young couples and young adults. Janet continues to live happily with the same man till today while she develops and improves, Janet determined to make the marriage and relationship in her life work. She consistently seeks for answers and solutions, praying and building her confidence.

I shared this story above because it resonates with me and from my past and present experiences, I became strong to know that forgiving someone does not mean it "didn't happen," forgiveness doesn't necessarily resume trust... just do your part toward reconciliation. I know through experience - when we choose to forgive and allow that to work within our hearts; cutting off every place where anger, hurt, bitterness, and fear, thoughts of self-pity or self-righteousness rise up then the event becomes nothing but a memory, we find ourselves free of all emotional attachment to it, we even forget it. We are able to bless those who have injured us with a sincere heart and are even willing to return to the relationship and build again what God intended to build the first time around. Some of your healing and miracle requires your forgiveness to yourself and to others. Let go, let them go and your miracle come in, Forgiveness lets you turn your back to bitterness "Forgiveness is giving up all hope of a bitter past." If you have a regret about something you've done, use this moment to forgive yourself. If you have resentment against someone else, use this time to forgive him or her. Things don't go as planned. Learn to forgive and forgive quickly. It will reflects your emotions and gives you peace, joy and successful.

I believe emotional breakdown, lack, frustration, the unknown, abuse of power, inferiority, insecurity, disappointment, discouragement, weakness, unfaithful and the influence of drugs/friends/family, anger and abuse will make a man, or a woman beat their partner/wife/husband. I believe there are solutions to these issues in relationship but first things first. They should realise and admit that they have problem and they should seek help, professional counselling, pastoral counselling, prayer, support, deliverance and willingness to help others with their testimony. With God all things are possible and there is nothing too difficult for God of the Universe to do. Sometimes we get involved in blame games, governments blaming parents for what is going on in society, drugs, killing and stabbing, gangs and rapists, parents blaming the government and the film producers, wives blaming the man that left them, the pursuit of money and career and even blaming the children that became rebellious and children blaming their parents for not listening to them and finally social services blaming parents and parents blaming them. No one is taking any responsibility of those actions or their actions. There are so many charities and groups and religious leaders that are working hard to find solutions but not enough and we try to push the main problem aside. There is no point dealing with the problem from the surface or from the top, but we must recognize the root of the problem, charity beginning at home, it is a generational problem and the earlier we start researching the issues and pay attention to details, the earlier we can help ourselves and help others. However, let us start with individuals, you and me and with this.

Remember life is too short; life can be hard sometimes, it is not easy with problems on our minds, and we have got to take one day at a time. Rome was not built in a day, it takes patience and better understanding and love to develop ourselves again. One that perseveres will not give up nor quit, though the sea may be rocky and rough, the Universe will make sure we see the lighthouse for you truly is a guiding star. No matter how far, He travels with us in all directions so we may overcome all our trials, tribulations and challenges of life. Yes you can and it is possible to be fulfilled and be successful in life and all things are possible. One of the reasons is when you don't understand the main reason why people behave a certain way, that could affect any relationship and the love to be lost. In my own personal experience, I found myself in a situation where I was about to make a decision in my life and I was in a state of giving up all my hopes, my fight to make all kinds of relationship work and prevent from crumbling and I didn't know what to do any more. Have you found yourself in a situation where you've given all your love to certain people and they throw your love in the trash including your value? And you have done all what you know to do or you found yourself loving the wrong person or the person that couldn't give you love back or abuse you financially, emotionally, spiritually? Are saying to yourself is it worth trying and you are in the midst of given up or quit like my situation? I went to so many seminars, meetings, counselling, read many books and listen to audio and watch motivational and inspirational videos to develop myself.

We have all made mistakes and fail in life however, we do not sit down, fold arms and lament on it or blame somebody, but own the responsibility and rise up, wipe our tears, face reality and fight back by turning the situations around and be encouraged, inspired, motivated, mentored, empowered and be transformed. After many seminars, conferences, meetings, webinars, Skype and telephone mentoring, retreats, networking, wisdom and training I received from my mentors, I decided to add more values to my life. My goals is to reach out to many homes, students, prisoners, women youths and leaders, to challenge and inspire, motivate and empower them. I have overcome, and succeeded in turning my situation around, forgive, love and show kindness and I am achieving, learning, improving, going places to share my stories and happy, then others can also - it is possible, I believe relationship is crucial in everyday life and there are different types of relationships issues, challenges, principles, and there is no problem without a solution, no gain without pain and no glory without a story and this is just an eye opener to many solutions out there to better ourselves in relationships and works of life. There are also many limitations that can hinder and jeopardise our happiness and limit us in succeeding but never give up nor quit the game of life, keep holding on your dreams and believe it and achieve it.

In nutshell, how did I bounce back, forgive myself and others, recover and reconnect? Personal development and mindset are key to everything. Self-Love - love myself first and love others. Face and overcome every adversity. Value myself and others. Enjoy my life and accept love and enjoy loving others, build effective communicating, commitment, focusing, connecting, networking and associating with people that are positive, like-minded and working towards their life goals. Making decisions and determine to take responsibility of my actions, not letting anyone or any adversity and challenges stop me, they could slow me down but never stop and never give up but keep striving and moving forward.

> *"Our setback will become our setup if we do not give up"*
> *Elizabeth Lucas-Afolalu*

One of the meetings I attended was Power to Achieve weekend where Andy Harrington the key speaker and organizer of this event drew my attention to the awareness of Coping Mechanisms. He explains that all of us have experienced moments of emotional pain and of course it's natural to want to avoid these situations happening all over again. As a result we can develop coping mechanisms whenever we feel stressed or challenged. These coping mechanisms cause us to experience the 3 D's. DELAY the inevitability of change. DENIAL that there is something that's not quite right in our world. DISTRACTION from the reality that our lives are not the way we want them to be. He explained further that there are many types of coping mechanism behaviour but they can be easily summed up as stemming from one of 4 character types Which he called the shadow selves: The Controller (dominates); The Pleaser (is dominated); The Analyser (retreats in their head) and The Busy Keeper (juggles) and instead we should find the warrior in us and lover, and jester and sage. From this I have better understanding of myself first and then others and how you and me behave to our loved ones.

Insecurity is forever locked in a cycle of jealously and anger. It's like a parent who's angry with their child because the child is having "too much fun". Instead of letting negativity build inside, learn to enjoy other's successes. It's a stupid fact of life. But our own happiness is extremely dependent on the way others perceive us. You may be in a relationship, but that doesn't change who you are. And that's where the problem starts. As individuals, we evolve and change all the time. You're not the person you were last year, and you won't be the person you are now next year. People may have their opinion about you but you don't have to listen, People can emulate or pull you down but you don't have to allow them to get to you and control your emotions and just ignore them and move forward. Stay secured on who you are, Stay focused on where you are going and what you want to become. Keep conscious of where your values lie. Know your value and raise the standard of your value. There are lot of layers of tension, stress, mistrust, dishonest distorted perceptions and unwanted baggage has been accumulated as we are growing older that we miss out the important. And we are far away from getting the health and right feelings and working on our beliefs. What do you believe about yourself and your situation? Do you believe the worst about every situation, or are you a positive person?

Help yourself to develop a positive mind-set. Then put your positive thoughts into action by going after and doing what you need to do to accomplish your goals.

> *"You've got to be hungry to achieve and succeed*
> *and be a better self and be happy".*
> *Elizabeth Lucas-Afolalu*

ABOUT THE AUTHOR

Elizabeth Lucas-Afolalu is the Award-Winning Author, Inspirational Speaker, Youths, Family and Relationship Adviser and Mentor. She has been recognized for her contributions to Humanity and Community and has been awarded, Author of Greatness, Woman of Excellence, The Legend Award, Inspiration and Relationship Award, Shine Ambassador Award, Award-Winning Speaker, Humanity Award. She has been featured on National Press such as Financial Herald, Fox News, ABC New and NBC News, Small Business Trendsetter Magazine, Okunsgroup Magazine, Victorious Life Magazine, Powerhouse Global Magazine and Local Hornchurch Newspaper. She was featured on Diversity Television and Amaze TV and has been interviewed on many media platforms. She is Founder of Time with Elizabeth Lucas, presently a Presenter on Radioiere Family Channel. She is an International Speaker at Powerhouse Dubai Summit 2020 and Global Woman Business London Summit. She shares her wisdom, incredible personal story and experiences. She has set up a programmed to help Youths, Relationships and Families in the area of Renewing Mindset, Building Relationships, Creating Kingdom Wealth and Personal Development in her Yes You Can Online Academy.

http://www.yesyoucan-by-elizabeth.com

CHAPTER 9

LESSONS FROM JIM ROHN

By: Izabella Niewiadomska

It's been over 10 years since Jim Rohn left us on 5th December 2009.

During his life Jim mentored many successful entrepreneurs, CEO's of Fortune 500 companies, leaders of global organisations and personal development speakers. Millions of people attended his live seminars, read his books and listened to his programs.

Knowing Jim Rohn personally and meeting him regularly over 18 years, was an honour and an incredible privilege. I feel lucky, thankful and blessed that I was able to take part in his live lectures, attend dinners and parties with him and learning how to be successful in business, and most importantly, how to live an extraordinary life.

When he spoke, his every word was a pearl of wisdom, and every sentence a quotable message to reflect on. Many of his quotes became part of my life, my personal philosophy and my way of thinking.

Although Jim Rohn is not with us anymore in his physical form, the wisdom of his words still influences people's lives every day.

For things to change, you have to change.
For things to get better, you have to get better.
Jim Rohn

When I first heard these famous words back in September 1992, I was not aware they were famous. I didn't know that Jim Rohn was an entrepreneur, author and world-renowned business philosopher, known by millions of people in almost every corner of the world. In fact, I had never heard of him until that day, until that very moment when his words were quoted by a man, smartly dressed, standing in front of a large audience in a hotel conference room.

Little did I know that Jim Rohn will soon become my mentor but I didn't know all that yet and so I was just simply intrigued by his words. Is life really that simple? Will things in my life change just because I will change? Will things get better when I will get better? Would changing myself be enough to change my reality?... My mind was racing with many questions.

I looked around the room and saw that most of the people sitting in the audience had this look on their faces that probably resembled mine. Their eyes were glowing with a mixture of hope and disbelief, as if Jim Rohn's words sounded a bit too good to be true. Were they? What if they were true? Oh, I really wanted them to be true. I really wanted things to get better in my life.

As the presentation continued, my mind drifted for a moment to a Sunday a few days back... It was a lovely warm autumn evening. A tall man standing outside a Polish church in Putney was handing out some leaflets. After 2 years of living in London I got used to a scene like that. Handing out leaflets on the streets was a popular way of advertising in those days. I was always curious to see what they were advertising. Maybe it was something I needed - something useful. You just never know. That's what so exciting about life.

This man seemed to be especially eager to give a leaflet to each person, and so I ended up with one in my hand, just like most of the people leaving the church that evening.

The leaflet was handwritten, photocopied, cut with scissors. At first, I thought, how unprofessional and then I smiled thinking that it was not the quality of the leaflet that mattered, but the words on it, and they got my full attention. Interested to find out more, I decided to call the number from the leaflet on the following day. Going to bed I was still thinking about the words I'd read. They sounded like a promise, a hope for a better future... Somehow the fact that I got the leaflet in front of the church felt like a good omen, as if the universe was sending me a helpful hand.

> **It not what happens to us
> but what we do about what happens**
> Jim Rohn

I grew up in a large city in Poland in a happy and loving environment of my family. My parents lived a comfortable life. Dad was a corporate lawyer, Mum a PA and a bookkeeper. Twice a year we used to go on a family holiday and life felt good. They are now over 80, retired and making the best they can of each day. Throughout their working life, they have never had a business, always employed, always working for a boss. My career plan was largely influenced by their career path – to have a good education and to get a good job. This was something that most people in Poland were aiming for back then. I did that too.

Loved my career, had a good salary, wonderful friends and great connections. I have a way of looking at things and seeing with clarity what other people sometimes can't, which can be helpful. Thanks to this I quickly became known among my friends and work colleagues, as a person to go to, when people got stuck with something and needed to resolve it.

Then when I was 23, a miracle happened – a true blessing in disguise that turned my life around. I became unwell through stress at work and nearly died. The experience put a new meaning on my career and on my total life. Health became my top priority and I had to make some lifestyle changes, to balance my health with a demanding career as a journalist.

A few years later, I decided to go to London, just for three months, to study English, as this could open new working opportunities for me. In 1990 Poland was not yet part of the EU and so I travelled to the UK on a provisional visa, which meant I had to show up at the border on a specific day, without any guarantee to enter the country. This used to be a normal procedure back then. The interview with an immigration officer at the border was a final deciding factor.

Traveling to the UK was slightly a risky decision because on the day I received my provisional visa, I learned that I was pregnant. I kept thinking: Should I stay, or should I go? Have you also been at crossroads in your life and not sure what to do, which way to go?...

Getting a provisional visa felt like winning a lottery ticket, I didn't want to miss out on the opportunity. On the other hand, the safety of my pregnancy was even more important. There was something pulling me towards London, an invisible force that felt good and positive. The challenge was to choose what to do.

I like knowing that each of us has been blessed with the power of choice, the most precious gift and best asset. No matter what happens, no matter what the circumstances are, we always have a choice. Even when you feel trapped and think that you don't have a choice, you do. It is the choices we make every day, in every moment, that influence the quality and the direction of our life. What's fascinating is that our choices are not final. Each day we can make a new choice, start a new chapter in life, adjust or change completely our direction.

It was easy to be fearful and use the pregnancy as an excuse for not going. I chose to trust that everything would be fine. I was going only for 3 months after all. I knew how to take care of myself and was confident that I can find my way in any situation, even when I was pregnant. My life experiences thus far, plus years of hiking in the mountains, and being a leader in a Polish Scouting and Guiding organisation taught me resilience and self-reliance.

I packed my bags and headed on my own to London. After 24 hours of travelling on a comfortable double decker coach and a scrutinising interview by the immigration officer at the border, I received permission to enter the UK. With a sign of relief and a happy smile, I went back to my seat on the coach, thinking that in a few hours I will be meeting with my great uncle, whom I met only once, when he was staying with us in Poland. He was going to wait for me in London and take me for a week to his home in Littlehampton.

London welcomed me with a surprise. When the coach reached its destination, my great uncle wasn't there. I watched all passengers being happily reunited with their families and friends. Soon everyone who was traveling with me was gone and I was the only one waiting.

I didn't mind waiting, but the heat was slowly increasing my tiredness. I was beginning to feel slightly frustrated and hungry. I wasn't worried. I knew there was a perfectly logical explanation for him being late.

What I didn't know was that my great uncle was waiting for me at Victoria Coach station and I was in another part of London, somewhere near Euston. He was waiting there, and I was waiting here, just like in the movies. If we both had mobile phones, everything would be easy, but mobile phones in 1990 were not a common thing yet. Sometimes I wonder how we survived without mobile phones.

Eventually, I decided to take matters in my own hands. Dragging my entire luggage I managed to find a hotel where I learned which station

I need to get to, to travel to Littlehampton, and arrived there on a train at night by myself.

The second surprise occurred a few weeks later. I faced a couple of health challenges which meant that for the safety of the pregnancy I couldn't travel and needed to stay in London until my son was born. My plan, to get back to Poland after 3 months, didn't work out.

On hearing the news my husband decided to come over to support me, living behind his career as a fully qualified veterinary surgeon. As a newly married couple, expecting their first child, being together as a family was important to us, far more important than the career or money.

After our son was born, I wanted to continue studying English and we decided to stay in the UK. There was no logical reason for starting a new life in another country. In Poland we had friends, family, connections, good jobs and great position in society. Here we had nothing. Here we were just a couple of foreigners who didn't speak English well.

It was like downsizing life on all levels. Our families couldn't understand it and I couldn't explain it either. Yet I had this gut feeling that something special was awaiting us here.

The beginning of our life in the UK as a family wasn't easy and straightforward. I guess, sometimes you must take the risk and cope with temporary difficulties if you want to follow your dreams. Trust your intuition. It always knows what's best for you.

> **The millionaire says to a thousand people, 'I've read this book and it started me on the road to wealth.' Guess how many go out and get the book? Very few, Isn't that incredible? Why wouldn't everyone get the book? A mystery of life.**
> Jim Rohn

As I was sitting in the audience, I realised that, out of all the people who were leaving the church in Putney the other night, I was the only one here at the meeting. Why none of them come? I didn't know. It mattered that I was here.

The words on the leaflet said: "International Company" is looking for bilingual people to help with the expansion of health and Nutrition Company into Europe". I was fluent in Polish and Russian and could speak basic English, passionate about health. In my mind I felt qualified for this business opportunity that potentially could completely transform my life.

Although I never thought of having a business, I wanted to change my situation for the better. I wanted to gain financial independence, provide the best for my son and to have the freedom to do what I want and to live where I want.

I was inspired by the stories of people at the meeting, people from all different walks of life sharing their wellness and income testimonials. Some were from other European countries, so I thought, why not me?

The company was one of the leading health and nutrition companies with a beautiful mission to change nutritional habits of the world, person by person, country by country, language by language around the entire world. I liked that. I wanted to be healthier and happier myself and the idea of having a business and helping people to achieve the same felt uplifting.

I didn't know much about a network marketing business model but it was reassuring that the model was already taught at the Harvard business school. All I knew that it worked, it sounded simple and I thought I could do it.

It was a bold attitude, as I had no capital, zero business experience, no bank account, no credit cards, no connections and no telephone.

However, I had a willingness to learn, a desire to make a difference in the life of others and make my life better, and I was not afraid of hard work. I liked that my success was dependent entirely on me and it was up to me how fast or slowly I will build my own client base and a team.

The day I decided to join the leading health and nutrition company I became a leader of my own business. It was one of the best decisions in my life. I was buzzing with excitement.

I started very part-time working from a payphone and in my first month I qualified as a supervisor, a first step on the company leadership ladder.

> **Don't wish it was easier, wish you were better.**
> **Don't wish for less problems, wish for more skills.**
> **Don't wish for less challenge, wish for more wisdom.**
> Jim Rohn

Starting a business for the first time in your life is a bit like learning to walk. You want to run, but you must take the baby steps first. You must be prepared to fall often and don't be discouraged. We adults can learn a lot from observing babies.

Babies never moan, nor complain and never feel guilty when they fall. They just smile, get up and try taking another step. They don't quit. They just keep trying until they walk. Adults often expect instant perfection; they are too hard on themselves. Babies enjoy learning and making a progress.

At the time when I started a business we lived in small ground floor room and shared bathroom with other Polish people who were living in other rooms in this otherwise magnificent four story townhouse, located in the heart of London.

When the payphone rang, I would grab my scripts, one for the products, and the other for the business opportunity and sprinted along the corridor to pick the call. I wasn't even sure if it for me, but I wanted to be the first one to pick it up, in case it was someone calling in response to my flyers.

I had to accept that a payphone doesn't have an answering machine and I was going to miss some calls when I wasn't in the building or didn't hear the phone or when another Polish person from the building who didn't speak English took the call first.

When I managed to pick up the phone, some people were putting the phone down on me. Probably they were put off by my strong Polish accent or could hear that I was reading a script. I didn't blame them for that, although deep inside I was a bit judgmental and questioned their good manners. Now I know that it was never about them, it was always about me, my attitude and my skills.

I knew though that I cannot let people behaviour affect my emotions. I needed to maintain a good positive attitude for the next call. I'm grateful for each person who put the phone down on me, because they were fuelling my desire to get better. It was my beginning, and eventually I did get better.

What I needed to do, was to make up in numbers what I was lacking in skills! Put out more flyers to increase my probability to have more conversations and learn to speak better English.

One of my fears as a beginner in business was that people might ask a question, or use words I haven't learned yet and I would not understand their question, or that I would not know the best words to express my knowledge and provide them with an intelligent answer. Luckily, I quickly let go of those fears. As my English was improving, my confidence was growing, and I started to get more clients and more team members. I was attending regular weekly trainings and every day I was listening to my tapes with Jim Rohn.

Leaders must learn to discipline their disappointments. It's not what happens to us, it is what we choose to do about what happens that makes the difference in how our lives turn out.
Jim Rohn

Have you ever been disappointed? Have you ever had high hopes for something to happen, but it didn't, or not in the way you were expecting it to happen? Maybe someone said he would be on time, but he was late. Perhaps you expected to do well, but you've underperformed and didn't get the results you wanted.

Whether you are a CEO of a large organization or a team leader, or a leader of your business, or a leader of your family, learning how to discipline your disappointments is vital for an effective communication with others, it supports your happiness, success and your overall wellbeing.

Like many people, I've had my own share of disappointments too in both personal and business life. A man said, "I will come to a meeting" and then he didn't show up. Why did he not come? He seemed to be so enthusiastic, I thought, so interested in starting his own business and so polite.

In the early days of my business I was often disappointed when people didn't show up or cancelled appointments in the last minute. I used to wonder - Why is it that some people say one thing and do another, and some people do exactly what they say they would do? I don't know. It is a mystery. Some people do and some don't. Jim Rohn would say - "Isn't that interesting?"

Sometimes, I was disappointed with myself too, especially when I didn't reach a monthly target that I set for myself.

Later I've learned however, that being disappointed is not such a bad thing. It is in fact a valuable emotion and just like every human emotion, it is there to serve you. Your emotions guide you and tell you clearly what you don't like or don't want, and they help you define what you do like, what you do want or prefer.

The question is though: How long do you stay disappointed for? For an hour, a week, a few months, years or just for a few seconds?...

Jim Rohn's suggestion was simple: Learn to discipline your disappointments.

The faster you let go of your disappointments, the better for you, for your health and business, and for everyone around you. Either you will let your emotions be your master or you will be the master of your own emotions. It is especially important in the time of crisis.

One of my biggest business disappointments was when Poland was hit by a bad publicity about the company - I was an independent member of. It was an unexpected blow. Although the news was not true, press created a bit of a stir and within a month I lost 98% of my business in Poland. It was a big learning experience and a big dent in the income.

Thanks to the teachings of Jim Rohn, I quickly let go of my disappointment, embraced "no problem" attitude and put my focus on working locally and thinking globally. Was it easy? Not really, but it didn't make sense to focus on what was lost. I needed to focus on making my local business in the UK stronger and bigger, and not on trying to fix from a distance my business in Poland.

My husband didn't take the setback well though. As he was not working the business with me, he didn't understand that setbacks are perfectly normal in any business. They provide us with new learning and insights which allow us to grow and become stronger, wiser and richer in experiences.

When a few years later I read "The Cashflow Quadrant" by Robert Kiyosaki, I learned that the mentality and mindset of an employee is very different to the mentality and mindset of those who are self-employed, business owners or investors. Tony Robbins says that Success is 90% mindset and 10% mechanics of the business. I agree. It is how we think and feel that makes a difference to our results.

**Learn to be happy with what you have
While you pursue all that you want.**
Jim Rohn

I started my business with a desire to make a positive difference in the world, with big dreams to be successful and create a better future for myself and my family. I didn't know that it would take me eight years before I would be able to spread my wings and take a full advantage of the business opportunity. For eight years I was struggling with some legal, personal and family challenges. During that time, I was working part time on my business, attending trainings, nourishing my mind, refining my skills, learning new ones and never complained.

My biggest joy was working with my clients, helping them to get great results, watching their progress, getting in shape, having more energy, and delighted to see their transformation and happiness in their eyes. The same joy I felt when the members of my team were improving their lives, becoming healthier and happier.

One my biggest challenges were my financial situation. I didn't have any credit or debit cards, not even a cheque book and no merchant facilities to accept card payments. My business was based on cash in hand only. This was slowing down my progress as many people wanted to pay for the products with their credit cards, and I could only accept cash. It also meant that when I needed to order more products for my clients or myself, I had to travel on a public transport, to the sales centre at the warehouse outside London. Pay for the products with cash and carry all the products on my back in a massive backpack back to my house in London. Sometimes I had to make a trip to the warehouse twice a week. I did enjoy it though despite all the inconvenience. It was fun and I always met interesting people on the way. However, it was not the most productive use of my time to travel for 5 hours to buy the products. I just had to be patient and make the best of it.

I knew it was not going to be like that forever. I was grateful when occasionally my friends could give me a lift to the warehouse. It's amazing how times have changed and how much time efficiency the online and mobile banking, introduced into our lives.

When in the spring of 2000 my bank issued me my first cheque book, I was as happy as a child at Christmas. That meant I could use a system called "cheques on file" that enabled me to order the products over the phone and have them shipped to my address or directly to my clients.

Funny, but when I look back, every time I wanted to see the results of my work too soon, I head Jim Rohn saying: "Your income will rarely exceed the level of your personal development." So, finally I got to understand that every single day of my journey, every single challenge and struggle WAS essential for me to go through to get stronger and to develop the skills to help me to be successful in business and in life.

My glory day came in the autumn 2004 when I reached one of top three highest leadership levels in the business. I was going to be recognised on the stage in Bolonia, Italy during a European Leadership Weekend. Speaking on the stage was not new to me. I've been accustomed to public speaking for many years. This time however, I felt incredibly nervous. The emotions from all the years of my struggles were building up under my skin. Just don't cry, don't cry, I kept saying to myself.

I had 5 minutes to tell briefly my story and was desperately trying to remember the words I carefully prepared. I was a bit extra nervous knowing that Jim Rohn was sitting at the round table just in front of the stage and I wanted to do it well.

My name was called, and the backstage crew member guided me to the stage. It was huge! The bright stage lights were blinding me. I knew there were nine thousand people in the audience, but in this moment I could see only a few faces of people sitting at the tables in front of the stage. Suddenly my palms went so sweaty that I had to hold the mic hard, so I wouldn't drop it.

I started saying my story and was immediately interrupted by my mentor, the legendary leader in the company, who oversaw this section of the day. He knew the details of my story; details I wasn't planning to tell. Somehow in an uncanny way, he understood the power hidden in those details. So much so that he decided to override the program and what was going to be a five minutes story turned into half an hour interview.

My mentor used to be a criminal lawyer and he knew what questions to ask to reveal what he wanted me to share. When he pulled the strings of my emotions, I just couldn't hold tears anymore. I let them roll down my cheeks, down my neck. - Next time I'm not wearing mascara, I said, and everybody laughed.

With a smile and rolling tears I shared the ups and downs of my journey, including the parts when my husband got blind. When I got to the end of my story, I saw all the leaders getting up from their chairs and soon the whole audience was on their feet clapping spontaneously.

It was such an honour! I felt humbled by the unexpected standing ovation. Much later I realised that they were not honouring just my journey or me, but the invincible spirit that lived also in them, the spirit that lives in every human being, the spirit that never gives up, that supports you to believe in your dreams.

> **What happened even as recently as yesterday**
> **is no longer of consequence,**
> **unless we choose to allow it to be.**
> **What we have been is an established and unchangeable fact.**
> **What we can become is unlimited, boundless opportunity.**
> Jim Rohn

I learned over the years that our attitude, how we respond to people and circumstances depends largely on our physical, mental and emotional state, on our beliefs and values and on our personal philosophy.

Your life is affected by:

1/ How you feel about your past - What happened, happened. It's is in the past. No one us can change the past. We can only change how we feel about it.

2/ How do you feel about the future? - Leaders need to have a positive vision for the future, because the vision, together with their purpose, will pull them through challenging times and will pull them towards the future, towards the results they want.

3/ How do you feel about everybody? – Value people, appreciate them, and learn from their successes and mistakes. - "One person doesn't make a family. One person doesn't make a symphony orchestra. One person doesn't make a country. Each of us needs all of us and all of us need each of us." – Jim Rohn

4/ How do you feel about yourself? – All your relationships are influenced by your relationship with yourself. Know yourself. Be yourself. Believe in yourself.

**Let the views of others educate and inform you,
but let your decisions be a product of your own conclusions.**
Jim Rohn

As I'm finishing this chapter the whole world is still affected by the COVID-19 pandemic and the wisdom of Jim Rohn takes on a new meaning. A new world is being created in front of our eyes and in this new world, learn to think for yourself, not accepting straight away what's being said by others. Instead, take a moment to ponder, to reflect on it.

Life has always been a mix of difficulties and opportunities. The future is going to be no different. The only question is: How well are you prepared to handle difficulties and to take advantage of the opportunities?

Remember, no matter what happens, spring always comes…

<u>5 Best Jim Rohn's quotes:</u>

**Success is not to be pursued.
It is to be attracted by the person you become.**

**Work harder on yourself,
than you do on your job.**

**Always do more than you get paid for
to make an investment in your future.**

**Take care of your body,
it's the only place you have to live in.**

**There are two ways to face the future.
One way is with apprehension; the other is with anticipation.**

ABOUT THE AUTHOR

IZABELLA NIEWIADOMSKA at Total Wellness Izabella Niewiadomska - "The Energy Entrepreneur" Speaker, Award winning Author, Performance Nutrition and Wellness Coach, Health and Mindset Strategist, member of The Association of Transformational Leaders for Europe, Associate at the Royal Society of Medicine, Ambassador for Women Of Contribution, Nutrition Sponsor of the world record expedition, philanthropist, entrepreneur. Over the last 27 years, Izabella worked with thousands of people, in the UK and across Europe, speaking, training, coaching, helping busy individuals and organisations raise awareness about how what we think, what we eat and what we do habitually, impacts our energy, performance and our physical and mental health. Trusted with many leadership roles since she was a teenager, from the Head Girl of the whole school, a team leader in Polish Scouting and Guiding Organisation, to name just a few, to being Global Expansion Team leader in a business network marketing organisation, Izabella's developed her own effective leadership style.

Her Nutritious Mind Method transforms the quality of our communication and helps create thriving professional and personal relationships. "Losing my health through stress over 30 years ago, while working as a journalist, sent me on a quest not only to regain my health, but also to explore and study what really impacts human health and how this knowledge can help us achieve success without losing our health. Mentored personally by Jim Rohn, trained by a Nobel Laureate in medicine, Dr Louis Ignarro; by Dr David Heber, the Founder and Director of the Centre of Human Nutrition at the UCLA and by various world class experts to ensure her knowledge is at the cutting edge of the industry. Co-author of two No1 international bestselling books 'Pay It Forward Series - Notes To My Younger Self' and 'Transformation Lessons - 38 Insights to Manifest Your Best Life'. Her new book is 'Stop Dieting Start Eating - How To Look Delicious, Think Nutritious and Spice Up Your Life. Inspired by her amputee friends, Izabella started running at the age of 50 and went from an untrained runner, to now running 100k ultra-marathons, helping raise funds for Blesma, The Limbless Veterans Charity and other charities. Izabella understands that to live extraordinary, fulfilling life, you need optimum health, extraordinary energy levels and emotional stamina. It is especially important in the lives of busy professionals, leaders and entrepreneurs, as they also have many family oriented responsibilities in addition to their professional ones. Featured in magazines and on radio including: Daily Mail, Top Sante, Women's Fitness, Global Woman, Sovereign magazine, Powerhouse Global Magazine and Sky TV.

https://twitter.com/24Wellness
https://www.linkedin.com/in/izabellaniewiadomska
https://web.facebook.com/izabella.niewiadomska.7

CHAPTER 10

WARNING THIS CHAPTER CONTAINS "TRIGGERS"#

KEVIN HILL

Back through the swirls of time, in my early twenties; someone had a picture in their mind for me. It was a picture of an extremely battered bugle. It was then submerged into a river where the water ran over it and through it. When it was taken out of the river the bugle had no dents in it and was shiny brand new looking. It was ready for action, to give a clear Clarion Call. Little did I know at the time, that this was a process I would go through many times in my life. Life would throw many curve balls in my direction to knock me off course and off my game. There were times when I was relentlessly battered from every side. A bugle is the chosen instrument to sound a war cry. Life was like "OK! Get ready for the next battle, the next war!" I had not even realised that the last one had ended. It seemed at times I was constantly fighting, but times of peace and rest came. I had major road blocks and obstacles to overcome. And overcome I did.

The First Major Dent

The first major dent in the bugle came when I was only five years old. I do not have any memories from before I was five, but I do remember one day in particular. I was sat on the window sill looking down the long drive to the air base. My father was in the air force. Someone called my name. I turned round to see who it was and what they wanted. It was time to eat dinner. It was fish fingers, chips and peas. In the room was my twin brother, my sister, my older brother and someone else. My parents were not there. This was the day my father died. I grew up fatherless. I didn't have anyone to show me what it was like to grow as a man. I had no one to guide me through my teens or my adulthood. I did not know or could not receive a father's love at that time. However later on in life there were a couple of men who became father figures in my life and were able to offer support and guidance.

They say that, "It is always darkest right before the dawn." - Thomas Fuller 1650. My long dark night of the soul was just beginning. Dark storm clouds were beginning to form over my life for a monstrous storm that would last years.

Bullies Galore

"Get him", Bellowed one of kids in the gang as they raced after me. I charged down the road as fast as I could, but it wasn't fast enough. In an instant the boys encircled me, each jostling to have a go at me. I became a human pinball, bouncing from person to person. Their barbed taunts mercilessly shredded my soul. Getting tired of this they grabbed my school bag and rummaged through it. They took the stationery and divided the spoils of war. Pushing me down to the ground, they left, bemused that they had terrorised me once again.

I was bullied a tremendous amount at school. What made the situation even worse was the gang of bullies lived on the same street and the streets next to me. I was surrounded by bullies all day. Both at school and out of school they plagued my life. Back then, the teachers didn't really do anything about the bullies, there were too many of them anyway. The only place I was safe was in my own home outside of the area where I lived. Even as a teenager I had years of depression weighing down on me. The ever growing rejection oozed out of every pore.

Paradoxically, loneliness was my best and only friend. No one ever saw the brokenness of me living with the heavy relentless taskmasters of depression, rejection and loneliness.

A Dark Path

From the age of about ten onwards, I would often walk by myself thinking of ways I could kill myself. Lies had crept into my mind and heart and were poisoning them from the inside. These lies stuck and grew incessantly within me. Yes, even at that early age I wanted to die. I would go through different scenarios weighing the pros and cons of each situation. I would think about stuff like how quick or how painful each way to die would be. The lies began as a whisper but grew louder and louder until they screamed at me most days. The lies taunted me:

"You are not loved by anyone."

"You are useless!"

"No one will miss you when you are gone."

"You are worthless and will never amount to anything."

These lies became a driving force within me. There was no escape from their voices and fuelled by rejection and depression, things were soon going to take a nasty turn.

A few years later when I was at the tender age of sixteen I reached the point in my life that finally broke me. I had lost all hope. I was never good at getting up in the mornings. This one day I was late for work. I had left school and worked in an Ice Cream factory. I rushed off to work shooting a quick "Morning" to my mum who was in the chair. An hour or so later two police officers came to my work and asked to talk to me. Then came the devastating blow.

"Sorry son, your mum died early this morning."

I was so late for work I rushed out, thinking mum was asleep in the chair not even realising that she had died. This was the last straw. The fragile world of Kevin came crashing down. It pushed me right to the edge. I felt as though I had lost everything and was completely alone. At the time I had two brothers and a sister but still felt completely empty and desperately alone.

My mum's death just served to empower the lies and propel me closer to suicide. I had a friend who worked on lathes. He sharpened a lock knife I had. At the Ice Cream factory, we usually had our break time with at least one other person. However, this one particular day I was on my own. I had been taking the knife to work for a while now. Taking it out, I played with the knife for a short time then raised it up above my head. I brought the knife down on my wrist. At the point where I just nicked my skin, the words of a song from Jeff Wayne's, "War of the Worlds" came crashing in to my mind like a runaway train.

"There must be something worth living for

There must be something worth trying for

Even some things worth dying for

And if one man can stand tall

there must be hope for us all."

I was frozen with those lyrics reverberating around my head and the knife poised on my wrist. All concept of time disappeared. At some point those words entered me and my thinking began to change.

"Maybe, just maybe there was something worth living for?" I began to ponder. For the first time I could remember there was a glimmer of hope for me. That glimpse of hope was enough to keep me alive. I slowly folded the knife and slid it into my pocket, wiped and covered up my wrist and went back to work. I didn't tell my work colleagues nor my family and friends. No one knew for many years what had happened.

A New Hope

I still wandered round in a lost daze for over a year. Losing my job becoming unemployed and having no one to turn to, only highlighted how alone I was. Many people find something that helps them, for me it was finding out who I was and what my purpose was. For me this all began to happen when I had an encounter with God. I became a Christian when I was seventeen. It radically changed my life. I understood my identity in the one who created me as I became a "Child of God". The "War" was over and I could begin to rebuild my life. My purpose was to help people, especially children and teens. I have been building on that vision and goal since that time. Knowing my identity and my purpose has served as a pillar of strength that I can always lean on when getting battered by life's storms. That war had ended but there were many new battles and wars looming before me. For now, I was entering into a place of healing and rest.

From the time of becoming a Christian, Kevin the battered bugle was placed in the healing stream. It was a lot like the intro to a TV show.

"We can rebuild him. We have the technology. We can

make him better than he was before. Better, stronger, faster."

- Spoken Intro from "The Bionic Man" 1980's TV show.

New Challenges

The healing stream brought about its own challenges. I understood for the first time that I had to forgive people and this was one of the major keys in being healed. This was an incredibly difficult process to face up to and to do; that is to forgive those who have deliberately hurt you. Firstly, I gained an understand of what forgiveness is and how it works. Forgiveness is not understanding why something happened, but it is first and foremost a choice to forgive. It is not based on feelings, but they will come into play later. In addition to choosing to forgive, I learnt that if you do not forgive it is "you" who will still hurt, not the other person. Working through all of this, the person hardest to forgive was "Myself". After much struggling I was finally able to forgive myself for letting myself down and listening to all those lies.

Dark Storm Clouds Approaching

Another major ongoing battering was in the form of ominous dark clouds of depression. The best description of depression I have seen is where depression is personified as a black dog. If you have not seen it then search for it on YouTube. It is called: "I had a black dog, his name was depression." Suffice to say that depression has hounded me for most of my life. At times, especially when I was a child or in my teens I had major bouts of depression that could last weeks or even months. Depression robbed me of so much joy and enjoyment of life. There were not always reasons why depression attacked me but depression is a very stubborn critter.

Depression attacks your very core, it seeks to undermine everything about who you are and to stop you fulfilling your purpose in life. I am a very firm believer that everyone has a plan and purpose for their lives. Not everyone figures out what that is or how to appropriate that into their lives, but I believe it is there. The out working of depression is twofold and I have fluctuated between both of them depending on the situation. One way is to become a very negative person who wallows in extreme sadness and tends to lean towards isolation. They become immobilised and want to hide away from the world under their duvets. Their power and energy is zapped away, as is their self-esteem. They are rendered powerless. I know because I have drank from this cup and I have drunk the dregs of depression to the full. The other way is to appear the life and soul of the party; smiling and making others laugh like Robin Williams and so many others did. Both of these are ways to escape depression and are not the real you.

The real you is a small little person in the middle desperately trying to be noticed. If you give in to the hide away depressive side, then you will be filled with lies and self-doubt. If you go to the 'jolly everything is fine' attitude, then you end up just wearing a mask. There may be aspects of these that are part of your real identity. I am an ambivert. I can be loud and brash when I need to but I also enjoy being alone and quiet. These are part of who I am, however, I am not hiding behind the mask of either of these two sides. I challenge you to stop both of these and take off the mask. This is so scary but so necessary for your real identity to come out. You may need time to get to know yourself once again. The real you is much more capable of not listening to depression and the stuff it spouts. The real you is secure in its self-enough, so does not need to rely on depression to give it a false sense of identity.

Pressure, Under Pressure

Another thing that really loves to batter myself and others is stress. Stress and I have danced many a dance. Often stress takes the lead and trips me up during the dance. Stress and I have danced about family, life and death, work, money and so many more issues. Stress is not fussy at all, it will do a slow dance then in a flash speeds up to a fast up tempo dance, dragging you along either way.

It was not until I became a Life Coach that I started to understand what stress was and how it worked. Do you know that there are two kinds of stress? One is dangerous and deadly and will destroy you if it can. The other is good stress. WHAT? I hear you cry. How can stress be good for me? The only difference between a lump of coal and a diamond is pressure. The stress, pressure and heat that coal endures produces a beautiful, extremely strong diamond. Therefore stress and pressure is good for you and can transform you into a stronger, more resilient person. I compare bad stress to a "Black Diamond" where-as good stress is a "Diamond". I clarify this in much more detail in my courses about how to deal with stress. Once I understood that stress can actually be beneficial to a person it was easier to take over and lead the dance. Remembering that I am becoming a diamond that will refract the light through its many different facets is something that strengthens my heart. Yes, of course it is tough. No one likes to go through trouble, strife and stress. No one enjoys this process but understanding the final outcome far outweighs the trouble and hardship. You are being refined and transformed. Yes, YOU, and that is creating a far better person within you. We return to being a real and genuine person and knowing who that person is.

The "R" Word

There is a word most people fear and dread, even the mention of the word sends shudders down a person's spine. The word that carries so much fear and anguish is "Redundancy". I too wasn't exempt from this. This particular battering came in the form of a "Christmas Gift!" At a staff training meeting it was dropped on a few of us that we would be laid off. Wow! The actual end date was early in the next year but what a great Christmas gift to me and my family.

Have you ever been told something that is so twee and condescending that it makes you want to slap them in the face? Yeah? Me too! I was once told that, "You have not been made redundant, only your job has been made redundant." What a load of bull was my first reaction. Does he not understand the situation at all? I had lost my job and the ramifications of having no job and very little money, were hitting me hard. I had entered into a new battle, one of being unemployed. How would I be able to feed and provide for my family? Would I be able to get another job and if so how quickly? Was I a bad worker? Had I done something wrong or had I upset someone? This was a possibility, as I have being true to my calling of a being a Bugler giving a clear clarion call. Not everyone appreciates these outspoken words of "Encouragement!" All of these thoughts and issues were compounded by the lashing of rejection and that this became long term of unemployment. My confidence and self-esteem fell right through the floor down into the basement. Living? No, I was surviving in the basement of life. When I did manage to get a job interview I didn't get the job. These were jobs I could do blindfolded, one arm tied behind my back, riding a unicycle, while in a coma but did I get the jobs? NO, I did not. Which added fuel to the fire of the belief that I was not good enough.

The seeds of that twee saying were beginning to take root in me. What was it really saying? As I mulled it over enlightenment broke through my veil. When you, as I had done, put your identity into your work and job it is unstable ground. YOUR IDENTITY IS NOT IN WHAT YOU DO BUT RATHER IN WHO YOU ARE. Let that sink in. Most people fear redundancy because their whole identity is wrapped up in what they do: their job, being a house wife, their position, having and doing certain skills. If those things were taken away by redundancy, or lost, or something else, then that person is usually devastated. If, on the other hand, you are secure in your identity then you can overcome anything. "To thine own self be true" is a quote from Hamlet written by William Shakespeare. You cannot be true to yourself if you don't know who you are. Discover who you really are so you can stand steadfast in that knowledge and truth. There is so much power in fully knowing who you are and walking in that, when things like redundancy hit, you are not swayed. I have the power to overcome redundancy and all the trimmings that accompany it because I am Kevin Hill NOT my job.

What an Atrocious Year

Have you ever had a day or even a week where things seem to pile up on top of you? Well I had a whole year of this happening to me, and it wasn't that long ago. My year of 2018 started off in full fury against me. I was diagnosed as being "Neurodiverse by being Dyslexic". I knew that my spelling and grammar were bad but I didn't know why until this was revealed. Learning more and understanding what it means to be dyslexic, and how far that affects my life was an interesting journey.

Dyslexia is not just about problems with words. I learnt that my brain is wired differently and how I process things differently to those who are not neurodiverse. This presented me with all sorts of new challenges I had to adapt to. Being willing to change and adapt is a great strength that can be utilised to help build your character. I lived in Taiwan for ten years and the very first lesson that I learnt was: You have to be flexible like water. Water will flow where it can. It will go round objects or even eventually go carve through the obstacle to get where it is going. You need to be like water. A new challenge means I need to adapt and be flexible. OK no problem!

I was just beginning to wrap my brain around being dyslexic when the next wave hit me. One Saturday early evening my eyes started to go a little funny. I had double vision. "Hmmm!" I thought. "I think I will just lie down for a short rest." I did that but it did nothing for my eyes. In the UK we have a phone number, 111, which is a medical help line but not an emergency. I called that number and explained what had happened and was continuing to happen. They told me to go to the emergency department at the hospital right away. My wife took me to the hospital and we waited and waited and we waited and waited. Finally, I was admitted into the hospital however they were not sure what was happening to me. It transpires that I had had a stroke. You have got to understand that I do not do common. My stroke was a very rare stroke as it was right at the back of the brain not on either side of my brain.

While I was in hospital I was subjected to a plethora of tests and scans. The hospital took so much blood that I thought a vampire convention was in town. Someone had noticed something so a whole barrage of tests and scans were ordered. I had to have an endoscopy. That is where they use a camera and a tool to take a biopsy. The first time was OK, it just hurt a little when they pulled it out. I was called back to the hospital because they had done the procedure on the wrong area. So off I go the second time. The first time I was sedated and I asked for this again. It can't have been as strong as I seemed to be quite awake during this procedure. It felt like at any moment, the alien that was crawling inside me was about to burst out of my chest. Low and behold they were not satisfied with doing this twice I had to have a colonoscopy. It was "Dynorod up my Jacksy!" (Dynorod is a UK company that unblocks drains and 'Jacksy' is a UK slang word for a person's bottom.) I had no dignity left!

The results of these tests came in. I was in the room with one of the doctors. A student nurse was also present. The doctor in a very matter of fact voice began to talk.

"Mr Hill the results of all these tests have come back. I am sorry to say that you have Pancreatic Endocrine Cancer."

"OK! Erm! Can you tell me how...er..." I replied in a low shocked voice.

"How..er...long I have got before..." Lower my head and whispered. The palpable tension in the room was awkward. I continued speaking,

"Before...before I lose my hair?" The very serious doctor cracked a smile and the nurse laughed out loud. You see I am already bald and have been for many years now. We talked more and I left the room. I didn't go home, just found somewhere quiet in the hospital and I cried. My wife was working so I was alone at the hospital. At some point I stopped crying and made my way home.

BOOM! What a blow. The next few weeks and months were extremely difficult to process and I was very emotional. I shared with my wife and a little bit with my children. But the tests and scans and the drawing of blood didn't stop, in fact they increased. I just mentioned that I do not do common. I was told that Pancreatic Endocrine Cancer is also very rare. It is the same type of cancer that Steve Jobs had. It did not stop there. I was called in to the hospital yet again. This time they had discovered I had the very rare condition of MEN 1. This meant that I also had four overactive and enlarged parathyroids which also is life threatening. Whoa! I am now waiting to have surgery to have most of my parathyroids removed. The operation has been cancelled twice already because I have high blood pressure. One of my symptoms of MEN 1 is high blood pressure hence I need the operation to lower my blood pressure. I should have the operation in January 2020, just before this book is published and launched. The Pancreatic Endocrine Cancer is very slow growing and I am now on yearly check-ups for that. However, the emotional impact and fatigue are still contenders vying for my attention. Some days I am overwhelmed by a tsunami of emotions. By choosing how I respond to that each and every day is one of the challenges I now face. This is my daily walk and daily choice I have to make. Overcoming does get easier the more you walk in it, but that does not mean everything is hunky dory all the time.

I am very active doing my coaching, speaking and training across the globe. The second part of this year 2019 I have been to Paris once and Germany twice with a third visit in January 2020. I am not one to have a self-pity party for one. I shrug these things off and embrace life. I am so grateful and thankful to be alive and I endeavour to live life to the full. This is who I am.

As you have read this chapter you will have noticed a common theme running through it and that is the theme of "Knowing and Walking in your Real Identity". Your mind reset begins with knowing who you are. Your journey of overcoming first steps is gaining a deep knowledge of just exactly who you are. It is paramount in overcoming adversity. I read a cartoon comic strip of Charlie Brown and Snoopy. It said, "The growing soul is best watered by tears of adversity". I would add that in order for this to be effective you need to know who you are, recognise that adversity will come and embrace it so you can be refined. You cannot be an overcomer if there is nothing to overcome. There needs to be challenges and adversity in your life so that your character can grow. It is no use pretending these things will not come as that is not realistic. Life doesn't work like that. You could be one of the walking wounded, never forgiving and releasing that forgiveness. Ultimately you have the choice and power to overcome, to become the best version of yourself. That person knows their true identity and walks confidently in that knowledge. So will the real you stand up and walk in all your glory and power because you are an overcomer. I have overcome through knowing who I am, my faith in God and knowing that this lump of coal is being transformed into a diamond.

ABOUT THE AUTHOR

Kevin Hill is a "Resilience Expert" having overcome many varied obstacles and difficulties throughout his life. Kevin has also studied "Resilience" so that his work transforms, especially the youth as well as adults. Kevin is a multi-award-winning Speaker, Coach and a prolific Author. Kevin's easy-going style means he can connect with all ages and all backgrounds. Diagnosed as Dyslexic only a few years ago confirmed that Kevin sees things differently from most. This opens up the way for creativity to be released.

Kevin is married and has four children, he likes watching movies, chocolate and travelling.

Contact Kevin Hill via Email:
KHCTSinc@gmail.com
Or
https://www.linkedin.com/in/hillkev

CHAPTER 11

AWAKENING THROUGH ADVERSITY

By Omita Gaikwad

"I'm sorry to say, Omita, the results have come through and your thyroid cancer has returned." October 2019 saw the recurrence of my cancer that I had endured 21 years previously. Little did I know it would serve as my biggest transformation tool!

Right at the start of 2019 I had sensed a powerful shift happening and I knew big changes were afoot; an intuitive ability I have always been aware of since my early childhood. For the previous 5 or 6 years I had begun a more intense chapter in my journey of personal transformation. I was intentionally becoming more conscious of what was going on within me and around me. By the start of 2019, I had completed, what I believed, was a significant stage in (what some may call) my 'spiritual awakening'. I had accepted my entire self for who I was and had consciously decided to say YES to ME.

"Know from the depths within, that your presence has powerful purpose in this world " – Omita Gaikwad

In 2013, after the loss of my father, I was an exhausted, burnt-out and debt laden single mother, with no support network close to hand. My father was the one person whom, I felt, vaguely understood me. In the years leading up to his passing, I had endured more than a fair share of challenge and adversity. I had experienced childhood racism, discrimination, cultural and social exclusion, depression, cancer, car accidents, miscarriage, divorce, and resultant single parenthood. I had become a cocktail of emotional and physical turmoil.

Things reached a point where I said to myself, "No more!" I wanted to let go, not only of the pain from my loss but years of conditioning which had left me riddled with fear, guilt, obligation and insecurities. They had been holding me back from my greatest discovery. The discovery of me.

Amazing things started to happen. I came into a time and place of true surrender, significant emotional release and transformation. By 2019 I knew exactly WHO I was, WHAT I wanted to be and WHERE I needed to go.

"Clarity clears the way for powerful creative expression " - Omita Gaikwad

Many aspects of life had finally settled for myself and my daughter. We had successfully navigated the storms and had not only arrived, but consciously created calm waters. And yet, as 2019 progressed, I also sensed an element of exhaustion, but not like any of the physical or emotional exhaustion I had experienced before. This was different. It was more a heaviness in my heart, as though my soul was feeling trapped and suffocated. A beautiful bird in a gilded cage. Something was brewing within. My soul was YEARNING TO BE LOVED and was CRYING OUT TO BE SET FREE, not on a part time basis as I had been knowingly doing so, but completely. I knew I needed to align my whole self to my truth and my life purpose - of Global Upliftment and Transformation. But how? I had reached a mental block. Ironic, isn't it, how a coach shares energy and insight to help others set themselves free, yet here I was, stuck from within. Physician, heal thyself! Remember though, growth is a never-ending affair!

Having been through so much in my life, how could I, again, find the strength to release myself from my comfortable web of personal safety, control and security? I had sworn to myself I would never allow myself and my daughter to travel there again. Yet, here I was, on the threshold of one more new adventure. I knew I would need at least a good six months without having to think about bills, reporting in to a work schedule and juggling fifty things so that I could simply and entirely focus on my wellbeing, dreams and purpose. Deep, deep down, though, I knew that it wasn't just for six months that I wanted things to be like that. I want this for the remainder of my lifetime.

The heaviness within me was becoming unbearable. I knew what I had to do. I had to finally, once and for all, step out of my own way. I acknowledged in my prayers and meditation, 'I feel you soul, I hear your calling and now I am ready to set you and myself free. I trust in your plan, show me the way....' Instantly, just by the simple act of voicing those words to myself, I felt a huge sense of relief and lightness, as though someone had just removed a rock from my heart, that had been suffocate me.

"Unleash your wings, set yourself free and soar high into limitless possibilities" – Omita Gaikwad

Soon after allowing this shift within me, I began to get signs, repeated feelings and prompts. I had begun to see how I could move forward, a way ahead was being paved out and a light shone upon the path. This inner guidance was so strong that it could not be ignored. I handed in my notice in September 2019 to leave my job on 20th December 2019. Even then, the inner voice was getting stronger and stronger, repeatedly saying, "It's time, it's happening, things are going to unfold swiftly and powerfully. Trust what is about to materialise." What did it all mean? My left brain was, like, "How can things unfold swiftly? I still have three months' notice to serve? Despite feeling slightly confused and unsure, I still felt a deep knowing within me that everything was going to work out just fine. When I had previously experienced these powerful moments of personal shift, adversity had been around the corner! This time however, because of the 5 or 6 years of inner transformation and personal growth, anxiety or anguish did not overwhelm me. Within my self-transformation work, I had cultivated energy healing and more nurturing and positive habits which activated more relaxation, focus and grit. These included yoga and meditation, transitioning to a greener, natural and more nourishing diet, and regular exercise in the form of swimming, walking, and workouts at home. Mindset management and development was something I worked on regularly developing some really uplifting and powerful tools and techniques for myself.

"The deeper I journey within, the more meaningful life becomes"- Omita Gaikwad

I was, I thought, entering a more settled and balanced phase of my life, where health and happiness had now become a priority for myself and my daughter for the past few years, I assumed that everything was ok. Naivety (some would say innocence), nonetheless, has always been a consistent characteristic of mine.

My soul was communicating to me, my soul was guiding me, my soul was permitting me, once again, to put myself first and boy did I need this. So for those of you reading these words, NEVER EVER think that you are alone and as you begin to learn how to connect and become aware of your inner voice, you will always feel guided and supported wherever you go.

Through recent calm waters, I had begun dreaming again. I had begun feeling again and more importantly it felt as though after a very long time, I had started living again. And I loved every bit of it. Everywhere I went people respected me and accepted me for who I really was. I was noticed and acknowledged for those elements of my being that only I thought of in my dreams. And I wanted more….

My visioning became clearer, the intensity and clarity was so powerful, I could consciously feel the alignment within me and as with any type of growth, my physical surroundings now needed time to catch up and manifest in accordance with this. So, this small hurdle with my health, was to slow some aspects of my life down, so that other areas could catch up.

Genius, absolute genius, that's all I have to say about life and this universe – a truly powerful strategist!

The news about my cancer literally rolled in a few weeks after I handed my notice in, and as you can imagine, due to the urgency of addressing this, it wasn't long before I was on sick leave. Of course, momentarily, as I left the consultation room after having received the news from my Oncologist, I was numb and for a few moments couldn't think straight or even stand. I had to get some bloods taken in a room around the corner and the phlebotomist was talking away but it all felt like a haze, as though nothing going on around me was real. Somehow, I managed to make my way out of the building. My hands were shaking, my heart was racing and I could feel my eyes welling up. I saw a small wall and perched myself down on this.

"The cancer has come back, what is going to happen to my baby?

Who is going to look after her?

How is she going to cope without me?

What about once I go, who will sort out all of my affairs?

What about mum, the shock will be too much for her?

The doctor said surgery, who is going to look after my child whilst I go into hospital and after?

How will I cope with everything? And then treatment, how am I going to have enough money to safely get through all this? "

These were just some of the thoughts that flooded my mind and they were intense. But, as soon as I noticed that my vibration and entire emotional state had shifted into an anxious and frightened one and that I was spiralling into a negative whirlwind, I stopped. I took a deep breath and said – "this isn't you. You know that FAITH FINDS A WAY, and that the universe always has your back. There is purpose and growth in this. Embrace it, merge with it and expand. You said you wanted a big break, you said you wanted everything to change – well here the door is opening…"

My breathing began to slow down. I began to feel a little more reassured and found myself in a much more relaxed state.

I put my head phones in, played a spiritual playlist, and as I walked home continued to let go and surrender any need to control, so that I could once again acquire that much welcomed state of balance I would regularly find myself in on a daily basis. The transformation work that I had done on myself had resulted in a new emotional default where now feeling calm and balanced was my daily normal vibe. I began expressing gratitude in my thoughts for everything that I was blessed with - access to healthcare, the abundance of health I had access to in that very moment of sight, touch, hearing, speech, taste, smell and movement to say the least, endless possibility and my self-awareness. Gratitude is an incredibly powerful transformation tool that is always accessible to us in any situation and at any point in time. The more I focused on this the more ease I was able to experience. As always, the large park that I usually walk through when returning home from the city centre, gave me strength and inspired me, reminding me that no matter what weather comes your way, be it sunshine, rain or wind, when your roots are nourished with faith, you are able to stand tall and strong, just like the majestic trees I was seeing before me. The swans gracefully and elegantly poised guided me to keep my chin and head up high!

It was as though mother-nature was wrapping her arms around me saying "it's ok, I will always be here". By the time I reached home, although much calmer from within, the biggest hurdle for me was how and when I shared the news with my baby girl, although I knew my girl was strong and positive as we both had transitioned together in personal transformation efforts over the years prior to this and she too was a believer in the principle that EVERYTHING IS ENERGY. Sharing the news with my mum, however, who was a widow who lived by herself and had her own longstanding underlying health conditions, was going to need more thought and planning, as she had also developed mild anxiety and didn't have much emotional tolerance within her given her own journey through a range of her own adversities.

My baby girl arrived home from school, she went about her normal routine, got freshened up and changed and came in the living room to eat her afternoon snack that I would usually have ready for her on the days that I was either not working or working from home.

We sat down and I asked her about her day, she shared everything about how her teachers were, something funny that one of her classmates had done and what she had for lunch. As she was finishing her snack off, she then asked me how my day was. I told her that I had my appointment with the Oncologist and she wanted to know what they said. Until then I had felt composed and calm about the situation, but as I began telling her that they said the cancer has come back, just having those precious innocent angel eyes look at me, my eyes couldn't hold back the tears. I tried, but they needed to fall. If I had been able to keep them in just that little bit longer then maybe that would have stopped my little angel from doing the same. It had been so long since she had even cried, I forgot how it just pierces a mother's heart when you just want to take the pain away from your child. And I was a mother who had shielded, protected and raised this child single handed, yet I felt helpless. With one hand holding her plate and the other holding her snack close to her mouth, an ocean of tears streamed down her beautiful face.

I realised we needed this moment to release, so that we could let in our feminine strength that we would both need in the days ahead. I put my arms out and she came and held me tight. As I stroked her hair and wiped away my tears, I asked her why she was crying, and she replied "because your cancer has come back". I then responded "but we know that the God is always looking after us don't we?" She nodded her head, whilst still pressing herself against me tightly. "We have always known that it was a possibility that mumma's cancer or some other illness may occur because of the extra stresses that mumma has had to go through. And before you say anything, none of that stress has come from you, as it is your presence in my life baby that has taught me and given me the strength to be happy." We then held each other even tighter. " You know, that our lives are only getting healthier and happier because of the choices that we are making to be as positive as possible with whatever happens each day, right?" she nodded in agreement. "For both of us, so whatever appears to be going on has to be a part of creating what we want." She then released her grip a little, and began to confidently join the conversation. "Maybe now you can really focus on you mumma, and maybe you needed this to help you do that "she suggested so lovingly. "Exactly princess, that's my girl. This is who we are – super strong divine warrioresses! Something really amazing and magical is going to come out of all of this." She nodded with a smile on her face. I then asked her, "is my princess ok? "and she replied "YES". I can't begin to tell you how much strength I get from my precious child. Many a time we as parents are lost in the assumption that we must be stronger and knowing more than our children simply due to the fact that we are older in age and bigger in size (for some), yet when we choose to learn and grow WITH our children, we are reminded that we are only guardians there to protect, provide and support our children to be the beautiful beings that they are born to be. And whilst doing so, transition into even more beautiful beings ourselves.

She then went on to asking so what actually does this mean what needs to happen and I began explaining that I will need an operation in my neck to remove whatever nodules they have found and then after that will probably need radio-iodine treatment. There were questions about how we will manage and I did say that when we find the right time to tell her nani (my mother) hopefully she will be well enough to be able to come and stay with her whenever I needed to be in hospital. I did then go on to discussing that I was going to need my princess to become even more stronger than ever before, as she was aware of my mums health and agreed that we both needed to handle this calmly and wisely reassuring my mum that we are fine and everything was going to work out ok. I have to say at that moment that, I was always so grateful for the gift that my daughter had been in my life till then, but I was now more honoured to be her mother, as from then onwards, that young girl didn't look back once and since then has transitioned and transformed into an even more beautiful, inspiring, resilient, healthy and joyful young powerhouse lady!

This is how much power our presence, state of mind and vibration at any given moment can not only have on ourselves but on those around us also. Whatever circumstances may arise, how we choose to perceive them will determine how we journey through them. I believe that there is no right or wrong, no good or bad. Everything just is, and dependent upon whatever emotional state we are in each given moment, that will influence how we interpret what is going on around us. Some may say, but what about those who have done something bad or committed a horrible crime, how can you say that is not wrong? I wouldn't wish to position myself in a place of judgement, but based on the state I am in right now as I write these words, I would view the circumstance and individual with deep compassion and calmness, looking beyond their immediate actions and looking at how more love and upliftment can be directed to that situation, knowing that each and every one of us yearn for the same thing, happiness and acceptance. How we acquire this is different for all as we all have our own unique story and experiences to share.

The return of my cancer was a blessing, just as it had been 21 years ago. I began to notice a pattern. Every time I needed some sort of escape route from a place I know I had grown out of, something reasonably drastic (mostly relating to my health) would occur, swiftly directing me in another direction.

Everything just flowed even more for me since that time. What I could have turned into a huge mountain that I had to struggle to climb and overcome, became an opportunity to embrace with ease, faith and gratitude. During the time off, prior to my surgery, I entered a deeply soul-aligned state, connecting with my core and rediscovering what I truly desired, and then gracefully made my body, heart and soul my priority from then onwards. I had never felt more alive. Self-liberation is beyond words as you enter a realm so magnificent, magical and momentous that no matter what goes on around you, heaven always feels as though it is on earth. My operating system had a new default, almost like resetting to your factory settings, where you are wiped of any unnecessary programs.

I had finally become reconnected to, and intimate with my personal GPS or inner guidance system. Now aware of its functionality and knowing how best to operate it, navigating with intention has become so much more powerful.

"Envelope yourself with self-love and care and enjoy watching yourself bloom" - Omita Gaikwad

I breezed through surgery, mum miraculously was available and well enough to support as best as she could with my daughter whilst I had to go into hospital and upon my return. Although there were also many other angels and beautiful people who stepped forward offering support if we needed it, some close by and some, such as my brother and sister-in-law afar, ensuring that my daughter experienced as little emotional disruption as possible was a priority and being able to stay in her own home in a familiar and comfortable environment with someone she already knows and where she could also see that I was ok, would help her so much more in continuing with her everyday activities.

It appeared as though I had entered a state of continuous synchronisation with my soul's desires, or what some may call endless miracles. Everything that I had attuned to internally, every deep desire and dream, began materialising in some shape or form in my life, with ease and minimal effort, simply through my intentional focus and attention.

Volunteering was something I had always entertained since a very young age, and of late my intentions to want to do more through volunteering on a more global scale supporting those causes that were not only near and dear to my heart but would also allow me to share my personal experiences, knowledge and professional skill-set, the opportunities to do so gracefully glided my way. My dream projects, transformation coaching business and way of life were taking profound shape. I began simultaneously attracting connections both offline and online with uplifting and inspiring souls who recognised the truth within me and whom I could affiliate with to creating more collective upliftment and positive change across the world. One such beautiful soul, is Lady Anita Bradshaw, who presented me with this very opportunity to share some of my experiences alongside other beautiful and bold souls in this book.

I have always been driven, throughout my life, to finding ways to uplift others and spread more love and light in the world. In my younger days, my mum would repeatedly say to me, that she never entirely understood why I felt the need to care for the wider world so much, tirelessly searching for opportunities to serve. She'd go on and say, "Why do you feel as though you have the whole world's responsibility on your shoulders?" and I would reply innocently, "It is because we are part of one world mummy and this world belongs to all of us…". That drive and need to experience oneness, has always been my guiding north star, however faint and distorted the signal may have been at times.

The recurrence of Thyroid Cancer would serve as my biggest transformation tool. It enabled me to set my whole self free on my authentic path of truth, life-purpose and much deserved abundance. I had asked to be set free, and I had little alternative BUT to TRUST

THE UNIVERSE with every particle of my being, sit back and literally enjoy the ride. Something which I would not have been able to do so easily, once upon a time.

Today as it stands, my Holistic Transformation Coaching is a rich blend of many years of study, learning and personal practical experience with a strong user focused acumen, enabling me to truly connect on a deep empathic nature with my clients. I was directed through my own personal circumstances and studied and became certified in a wide spectrum of areas: NLP, Performance coaching, Naturopathic and Clinical Nutrition, Stress Management, Energy Healing and Happiness, Yoga and Exercise for Wellness.

Yet it wasn't that all of these positive efforts were time wasted and served no purpose, quite the contrary. Many a time we create an expectancy that when we are doing all the 'right things' nothing wrong can ever happen. But perception, is in the eye of the beholder, where WE CAN CHOOSE to associate any meaning we desire to any situation or circumstance. After all what is right or wrong?

"Widening our lens of perception, allows us to see endless possibility" – Omita Gaikwad

This was the time for me to actually experience the transformation that had taken place within me. To know how much more resilient and powerful I had become. To realise that my fundamental philosophy that EVERYTHING IS ENERGY, is true in every sense. This was the time for me to really step into my personal power and growth. And the only way to be able to assess oneself is through some form of test, right? So, this was, simply, another time for being graded by the University of Life. Although I do feel like I have successfully achieved and passed my PHD from this institution!

Now, to be living and aligned to such meaningful experiences which, had been set in motion through day dreams, even as young as a child and throughout my adolescence leave me awestruck, every single day. How truly spectacular and extraordinary life really is on a moment by moment basis. Yet so many of us, both knowingly and unknowingly miss out on this depth of blissful living, due to our need to conform to pleasing others', and lack of self-awareness of just how deserving we all are.

At first, I was completely overwhelmed by this mystical love that life was showering me with. It was as though the universe had wrapped its arms around me, reassuring me that I never had been, and never will be alone. Then, my feelings and understanding of my personal significance were magnified and elevated to a whole new dimension. I no longer felt overwhelmed. I, not only knew, but also completely believed, that I was deserving of anything and everything. This was the result of investing in myself, in embarking upon a journey of intentional and powerful personal transformation.

I had chosen to awaken through my adversity and now I was finally being ME…..

"I choose to glow wherever I go" – Omita Gaikwad

Thank you for taking this time to learn more about my existence and I wish you endless abundance of joy, health, happiness and purpose in yours.

ABOUT THE AUTHOR

Omita Gaikwad is a Holistic Transformation Coach, Speaker and Global Oneness & Wellbeing Advocate

Global Wellbeing and Oneness is her mission and this can only be accomplished as each and every one of us awaken and align to our authentic powerful true selves and become whole once again.

Self-awareness and personal transformation are the keys to unlocking, harnessing and experiencing true potential, happiness, health and limitless power, as discovered by Omita Gaikwad as she traversed and crusaded through varied periods of adversity such as divorce, depression, anxiety, loss, debt, burnout and cancer twice as a single mother.

Now having awakened through her exhilarating journey of self-transformation she has merged and blended her professional skills and life experience and embraced her life calling as a 'Holistic Transformation Coach and Speaker of Upliftment'.

Enabling individuals and organisations, through her coaching, in bringing more balance, sustainability and optimisation into their lives, with a key focus on Wellbeing, Mindset and Purpose to then transform them into the most incredible version of themselves is what makes Omita feel alive.

Social transformation and Global Citizenship lies at the heart of her life and ever since she was a child has engaged in social philanthropy and spreading love and kindness across the world, volunteering her time and energy with a number of non-profit organisations on both a global and local scale.

"One You, One Love, One World" – Omita Gaikwad

You can follow and engage with Omita on the following social media platforms:

Facebook, Twitter, Instagram and LinkedIn @ **Omita Gaikwad**

To learn more about her Holistic Transformation Coaching and Speaking services please visit

www.puretransformationcoaching.com

CHAPTER 12

"SELF-WORTH LEADS TO SELF-LOVE"

by Sabrina C. Nelson

I believe that we have been put on this earth for a greater purpose – to utilize our greatest gifs and talents to serve others and share our vision with the world. Collectively, we all have significant contributions to make on the planet throughout our lifetime. Our vision is one of the greatest gifts we can offer to others in the spirit of "giving". It may be something very small or extraordinary that will make a meaningful impact in people's lives.

At an early age I was taught to show kindness and compassion toward others; whether they were family members, friends, associates and even strangers. Ultimately, I always felt compelled to make a difference in many people's lives at the expense of my physical, mental and emotional well-being.

I can personally attest to feeling a lack of self-worth growing up although I was raised to be independent and excel in every area of my life, basically my parents were grooming me to become an overachiever.

Also at the age of seven years old my parents realized I loved, dancing, playing the piano and several years later I learned how to play the clarinet. Eventually, I began performing in talent shows and I truly loved demonstrating my talents and fully engaging an audience. I had grown accustomed to winning in my category and age group.

However, that dreadful moment occurred when I came in second place, and this was certainly a pivotal moment in my life. My father explained to me, "Even though you didn't win, I'm proud that you tried your best. Understand that you don't need validation from anyone."

I appreciate the guidance my parents provided but they only taught me what they knew and sometimes people have the best intentions for you, but cannot grow and stretch you beyond their own perceived vision for you.

As I grew older it felt as though my heart was being stretched beyond the confines of the walls that had protected it for so long. I believe that **"self–worth"** is predicated on many different circumstances and a litany of experiences in our personal and professional lives that start from early childhood into adulthood.

For as long as I can remember, I've always had this desire to help others in need in some manner. I truly understood why people gravitated toward me and knew there was something unique about how I engaged others. Many people that know my heart have said; "You're such a people person, you'll even strike up a conversation with a stranger." Yes, it's true and this is partially the reason why I found my passion early in my life.

Throughout my youth and adult life I've always understood what my father had conveyed, but sometimes I still felt the need to continue exceling in many areas of my life to be accepted by my friends, family, colleagues, and even partners.

I developed this ***"disease to please"*** everyone and I paid a hefty price for continuing that behavior for many years. I was very good at providing counselling, compassion, guidance and support for many people in my life. But, I never allowed them to fully reciprocate the compassion, empathy and good deeds back to me.

Ultimately, it became very exhausting wearing a mask and trying to be strong for everyone around me but never making myself a priority. Eventually, I turned the lens of self-care on me but some of those same people would make me feel guilty, and eventually I would revert back to the same self-destructive behaviors.

However, back in 2008 the course of my life change forever. I had lost my oldest sister to cancer and six months later my father passed away from a stroke unexpectedly. It was the first time I had experienced an immediate family member dying. I was not mentally or emotionally prepared for my own grieving and healing process, but since I had helped other people it seemed as though everything would be just fine.

But, what I've learned is that healing is a personal journey and very long process for everyone. This surprised many people, but I didn't care about what they thought, it was now time to fully immerse myself into self-care and healing this deep wound and find myself again.

I decided to courageously begin walking down the path of self-discovery and the unknown in order heal as well as cure myself of the ***"disease to please"*** everyone. It took three years of painful inner work, periods of isolation, and introspection; then I eventually emerged like the phoenix rising only to discover my true purpose in life!

One day I heard a pastor say, "Whenever you are in the midst of a breakdown in your life, prepare yourself for a major breakthrough."

Afterward I began to understand what my true calling in life was and I pursued it wholeheartedly. I began thriving again in my profession as a project and facilities management professional, received numerous accolades, praise and compliments from supervisors, executive management and my peers. I was a consummate professional and enjoyed designing beautiful office space that fostered creativity, collaboration, and enhanced the communication with everyone.

On many occasions I started receiving comments about how I engaged people outside of the realm of my role. Colleagues and business partners began asking me for advice on how to emerge from a place of pain, fear and uncertainty.

At this juncture I started to become fascinated with self-help, self-development, coaching materials and started reading many different books, listened to podcasts, etc. from some of the most well-known thought-leaders in the world. I purchased numerous books by Eckhart Tolle, Louise Hay, Wayne Dyer, Tony Robbins, etc.

Also, I discovered that meditation could be a major catalyst to helping you focus on being fully present, cultivate "active listening" skills and provide a more fulfilling lifestyle. Then one day while watching Oprah's Super Soul Sunday, I saw a promo for Deepak and Oprah 21-Day Meditation Challenge; and that was the first time it dawned on me that meditation was one of the key elements to continuing my own transformation process.

I have heard it said that, "Anything we do for 21 days straight becomes a habit." I was fully immersed in meditating after day seven and have never looked back.

It became my life's passion to understand the fundamental practices of how and what makes people feel seen, heard and understood. Learning and understanding different communication styles (verbal and non-verbal) as well as thought processes. How to create our personal reality and how we can get more connected to our heart and our soul so that we may live with more contentment in many areas of our lives.

Fast forward to June 2013, the company that I was employed with for almost fifteen years was acquired. I was faced with another major cross road in my life, but this time it felt very different. Armed with the knowledge gained from my past, I was able to lean into the unknown and assist many of my colleagues when they were feeling uncertain about their future.

In late 2014 the time had come for me to exit the company, it was a bittersweet moment; and in the midst of this life-changing event that was happening to me my only brother suddenly passed away -- it was totally shocking because I had spoken to him three days prior to his death.

Now that dreadful grieving process was back in full effect. For the first few months of my unemployment I was able to fully embrace the grieving process of losing another sibling.

I had been down this road before but this time it was very different because I did not have a job to create a major distraction or at the very least stall my healing process. As you could imagine I was in a fog mentally and emotionally, I just allowed each day to unfold in whatever manner I was supposed to experience that day.

I literally forced myself to fully embrace this painful new chapter of my life. But, I realized that I did not want any meaningless distractions in my life going forward -- whether it was friends, partners, or family members leaning on me to assist them in some area of their lives.

One day I got still and had a deep introspective moment and thought about 'how do I want to impact the world going forward.' I have always been told that I should write a book. I started writing blogs to motivate, encourage and inspire people – although I was unemployed.

Also, I worked at SCORE a non-profit organization and became a Certified Mentor. In my role I provided established entrepreneurs and new entrepreneurs valuable business advice, shared tools to help them become more confident in their area of expertise, mentoring and coaching sessions as well.

Many clients started telling me that they felt different after our mentoring and coaching sessions, it was an overwhelming feeling of empowerment and confidence. They conveyed that spending time with me really helped them to really strategize and develop their business strategy for long-term success not just immediate gratification.

Ultimately, this was a major catalyst that inspired me to obtain my coaching certification. I delved into these courses with an extraordinary coach that held all of her students accountable for completing the assignments, exams, etc. I made the financial investment in myself and never doubted that I would succeed. I remained committed and dedicated to accomplishing this milestone in my life.

After receiving my Certified Professional Coaching (CPC) certification, it felt rewarding and I was ready to coach and motivate the masses, as well as assist with transforming their lives!

Ultimately, I began broadening my reach and started motivating people on social media -- via Twitter and Instagram. At first, this was daunting because my only exposure to social media was on LinkedIn.

But after posting messages on a frequent basis, I started receiving comments on my post and direct messages from like-minded people, coaches, and people from different walks of life. All of a sudden I began to realize how my motivational posts and words of wisdom were resonated with so many people around the world!

I'm a true believer that no matter what I've been through in my life, the moment I discovered my calling and purpose it has propelled me into becoming the "best version of myself."

As you can see my life story has highs and lows but I'm here to tell you that when you tune out all of the mind chatter, the expectations of our family, friends, spouses and colleagues you will become clear about what serves our highest good.

Yes, sometimes you will remain in your cocoon long enough to have numerous introspective moments, epiphanies and some AHA moments too!

Once you've tapped into your truth, ultimately you will emerge as your authentic self and be ready to soar like an eagle -- embrace the new version of yourself unapologetically.

Also, I believe that self-worth is directly linked to three words, Potential, Passion and Purpose: which are my three key pillars for transformational coaching.

Now, I would like to guide you through your self-worth journey. The moment you emerge as your authentic self you will have a clear understanding of your what's your greatest potential.

Once you discover your potential, I believe that your confidence will soar. But the key is to align it with whatever you are most passionate about in your life. When we have something to look forward to every day it creates a sense of being, momentum and gives our lives real meaning.

When you align your potential with your passion utilize this to find your "Why" and then you'll discover your purpose and calling for your life. Please understand that no matter where you are in your unfolding life journey -- just know that *"**You Are Enough**"* in this moment and will be enough tomorrow and every day moving forward.

To all the amazing, courageous and multi-faceted people all over the world – you are truly deserving of being seen, heard and understood. It's my hope that by sharing my words of wisdom with you, it will be a source of encouragement & inspiration while on your journey to becoming the *"**best version of yourself.**"*

If you cannot change a situation then change your perception of it. Eventually you will stop being a prisoner of your past and become the architect of your future.

You can accomplish anything if you are willing to **P.U.S.H.**, which basically means – "Persevere Until Something Happens."

Always remember that everything that has occurred in your past has led you to the *"present moment"* – you were uniquely created to fulfil your life's purpose. As you surrender to being fully present, you will experience your life blossoming in so many ways.

Someone once told me, ***"Turn your wounds and failures into wisdom. Use those life lessons as stepping-stones while traveling on your path to success. There is a blessing in every lesson."***

Do you realize that every time you were being rejected, it was actually an indication that you were being re-directed to something more fulfilling because it's for your own protection?

As you continue on your journey of **self-awareness and self-love**, you will discover so many unique and extraordinary things about yourself. Once you realize this important aspect of who you truly are in this world, you will look in that mirror and love every part of yourself -- and that is such a wonderful feeling.

When you love yourself completely and unapologetically you will never lack love. If other people don't provide that same level of compassion and love toward you -- well it's okay because you have a waterfall of love flowing within your heart and soul.

Like a butterfly, you become this beautiful infinite being that has tapped into unlimited potential and soaring to new levels. Now you are equipped with a different mindset to succeed going forward.

> ***"We delight in the butterfly, but rarely admit the changes it has gone through to achieve that beauty." ~ Maya Angelou***

This is one of my favorite quotes of all time and these words have certainly made a huge impact my life!

Please understand that when you focus more on loving yourself first, there will be people in your life that will not support you on your journey. At first it might feel hurtful and even strange, but if they cannot root for you to win then it's obvious that relationship is not worth salvaging – simply give them the ***"gift of goodbye!"***

What I have discovered about this journey called life is that, ***"self-worth is the highest expression of self-love."*** It's imperative that you remain true to yourself, stay focused on your life goals as you continue to create a "new version" of yourself. Always make your well-being the number one priority. When you invest in the growth and transforming yourself, you will ultimately reap the benefit of your wise choices.

Whenever you find yourself doubting how far you can go, just remember how far you have come. Reflect on everything you have faced, all the battles you have won, and all the fears you have overcome.

Appreciate where you are in your journey, even if it's not where you want to be at this moment. Remember that every season serves a purpose.

If you take more risks and make those giant "leaps of faith" you will become unstoppable! Your life will be transformed in such a way that it will astound you!

I love this quote; ***"The greatest act of courage is to be and own all of who you are, without apology, without excuses and without masks." ~ Debbie Ford***

When you are walking in self-love and show up in the world as your unique self, you will realize that your value will never decrease based on someone's inability to see your worth.

You know life is the most difficult exam, many individuals fail because they try to copy and emulate other people. But what they don't realize is that everyone has a different assignment and questions to answer, that's unique to their circumstances and life path.

If you are given a vision, it's because you are equipped with the skill, wisdom, knowledge, and talent to execute it. Never discredit your God given abilities.

I believe the whole point of being put on this earth, is to thrive in many areas of our lives and not just survive. But most importantly, to evolve into the complete person you were intended to become.

I implore you to walk confidently in the direction of your dreams, remember that setbacks are springboards to major comebacks. Failure is not fatal; delays are certainly not denials and life your life is a journey not a destination.

I posted the following quote on social media and it resonated with so many people, which truly warmed my heart. ***"When you look at your life as a motion picture, you become the producer, director and lead actor in the unfolding story of your life."***

One of my favorite mottos is: "Live on purpose and with a divine purpose every day!"

<u>Let's Stay Connected</u>:

Visit my coaching website: transformational-lifecoaching.com
Email: <u>snelson@transformational-lifecoaching.com</u>
Follow Me: Instagram: @scnelson007 & Twitter: @scnelson017

ABOUT THE AUTHOR

Sabrina C. Nelson, PMP, FMP, CPC is a compassionate philanthropist; dedicated mentor, certified life coach, motivational speaker, published author, blogger and volunteer. Ms. Nelson is a proven industry leader with over 25+ years of experience in real estate, facilities and project management.

Ms. Nelson is committed to building communities through advocacy, innovation, strategic planning, and volunteering with institutions and organizations that are committed to uplifting and empowering the community. She also dedicated to supporting underserved communities. As a volunteer

Moreover, Ms. Nelson was devoted to supporting the next generation with becoming better versions of themselves. As a visionary member and mentor through the Step Up Women's Network (SUWN), she inspired young women to abandon their fear and pursue their academic and career goals wholeheartedly. Ms. Nelson was also engaged in the "Pathways to Professions" workshops; which provided opportunities for professional women to lend their knowledge, expertise and guidance to enrich the lives of low- income teenagers in need.

Ms. Nelson is a certified Project Management and Facilities Management Professional. In addition, she is a Certified Non-Profit Fundraising Executive and also holds a Certificate in Creative Writing and Journalism from New York University's School for Continuing and Professional Studies.

She has been coaching individuals in their personal and professional lives throughout most of her adult life, and several years ago year she received her certification as a Certified Professional Coach (CPC) with a highly accredited coaching institution. She now provides coaching services on her website: www.transformational-lifecoaching.com

Ms. Nelson received the VIP Women of the Year award from the National Association of Professional (NAPW) for excellence, leadership and commitment to her profession, while encouraging the achievement of professional women.

Also she received the Continental – Who's Who recognition of excellence with professionals and executives who have demonstrated outstanding leadership and achievement in their occupation, industry or profession.

Ms. Nelson's recent accomplishment was recognized while at the Powerhouse Global Conference in London (October of 2019); she received the "Life Coach of The Year" Award from this distinguished organization.

CHAPTER 13

INTENT AND BELIEF

By: Sandi Rich Saksena

I do not have any control over what actually happens except for that, I have full control over My will for Myself, My intention, and why I'm here. That's all that matters

"Your biology doesn't spell your destiny, and you aren't controlled by your genetic makeup. Instead, your genetic activity is largely determined by your thoughts, attitudes, and perceptions. Epigenetics is showing that your perceptions and thoughts control your biology, which places you in the driver's seat"

Bruce Lipton Biology of Belief

In retrospect this rings true of everything in my life.

I grew up a much-loved child, happy and content, I don't recall having to struggle for anything, things just came my way, smooth sailing…

All I wanted came to me because It was never about conscious 'manifesting' as we talk about today. It Is my Being in my Subconscious.

My first instance where I was made aware of my 'over confidence' was when I applied for a university seat at one of India's top ranked women's colleges Lady Shri Ram College in New Delhi. I got the interview letter and, armed with my brand- new college 'trousseau' excited and enthusiastic about experiencing college life, I arrived for the interview, which I considered a mere formality! I was met by a sea of anxious faces and I thought why do these females look as if they've got their knickers in a twist? I was asked to which other universities/colleges I had applied to, I was taken aback, I responded that I wanted to go to LSR so why would I apply elsewhere? So, is ignorance bliss? I hadn't the faintest clue that I should have applied to other colleges no hedging my bets, no plan B! Needless to say, I graduated from LSR!

I flowed from graduation to marriage to motherhood - that is what I had wanted especially motherhood!

Surprise, a mother of 2 children an emergency gall bladder problem led to an ultrasound... Viola discovered Unilateral renal agenesis means that as a foetus I developed only one kidney. Found in roughly one in 1,000 lives. WOW! I am one in a thousand births with this! In layman's terms I don't have a left kidney and had a half a reproductive system. Anything is possible my genetic activity was/is largely determined by my thoughts, attitudes, and perceptions. I wanted so much to be a mom and I was!

I started my married life in Kuwait happy wife, happy mommy, immersed in my family. My happiness and contentment grew to dizzying heights as my husband's prospects improved by leaps and bounds when we moved to Bahrain. We were truly living not the good life but the amazing life. I had never seen so much money so many perks so much of everything. My husband and I come from middle class families that lived a good life on carefully planned budgets. At first, we couldn't even exhaust our furnishing and other allowances. It just seemed like way too much money! However soon the budget life style gave way to the splurge style and for 15 years it was easy street! People get used to anything in a year, 15 years this was THE LIFE It was could only get better.

My kids grew up in this it was the only life they had experienced, 5 star all the way – homes, schools, vacations, travel luxury living!

I was Snow White living in my dreams, in the passenger seat, (I had replaced myself as the driver of my life) on cruise control, oblivious, till we hit the worst financial roadblock, dead halt! Shaken from my slumber, I looked to my spouse to fix it! In short, I had given up on my intent and beliefs and handed over my well-being, my future to another person.

Dreams descended to nightmares as I set foot in Dubai. I was so immersed in my role as the supportive, dutiful wife I never questioned the move to Dubai, feeling secure in the knowledge that we would continue our journey onwards and upwards. The decision, the timing, impact, the repercussions, consequences nothing was discussed, I just accepted…. fait accompli. The contract my husband had signed fell through and with it our lives were thrown into turmoil.

Dreadfulness, anger, frustration, confusion, resentment, misery, type any of these into thesaurus and it still will not be enough to express the feelings we were experiencing. When one has been used to nothing else than luxury even a 20% drop feels awful, and here we were in free fall with no bottom in sight. No job, no money to cover rent, groceries and school fees. We were down to borrowing from my wonderful never questioning always supporting family. As all Indians do, I too bought gold jewellery to wear and enjoy, but never kept receipts as never in my wildest dreams did I see myself selling my jewellery. On my 3rd trip to the gold souk in Dubai I was told not to come back as they would have to inform the CID as I was bringing large amounts of gold to sell with no proof of purchase… You get the drift!

Seeing my kids being sucked into hopelessness, confusion, difficulty in concentrating at school and university, exacerbated my anxieties and fears for my family. What was most heart wrenching was what my kids underwent. They just could not understand what was happening their lives were being pulled apart, disintegrating at breakneck speed This lead to recalcitrant behavior in the extreme – rebellious, callous, obdurate!

Talk about relationships - well those were crumbling and unravelling! Marital bliss was now marital misery. Family life was full of angst, blame, games and more. We all react in different ways to trauma from the physical to emotional reactions. I lived in fear of creditors and eviction notices. My spouse was feeling disconnected and numb. He was suffering from insomnia, racing heartbeats, fatigue. We could not have a civil conversation he was edgy and agitated and ready to snap back all the time. He was feeling guilt, shame, self-blame withdrawing from others. The kids and I all were in shock, denial and disbelief. Anger, irritability, mood swings became a constant state of being in the house. He looked for jobs, business deals, consultancy any and everything. He even compromised ready to accept junior positions. It was my first experience of a 'cruel' 'uncompromising' 'cold' work world. No 'human' attitudes.

Things came to a head when he collapsed at a meeting and was rushed to emergency and admitted to ICU. I reached the government hospital and broke down when I saw him lying in the general ward for males still in his suit pant and shirt. This was a man who had had the top of the line medical insurance who had been treated only in the best hospitals no expenses spared and here he lay in a general ward because we had no money and no insurance. I felt emotionally and psychologically shattered and my sense of security was crumbling making me feel helpless in a precarious world.

For the kids and I all this happened unexpectedly I was unprepared for it. And worse still I felt powerless to prevent it.

Or was I truly powerless to prevent it? Introspection would come later the need of the hour was for me to step up to the crease and bat for the innings of my family and me! I was going to get a job and contribute to our financial welfare.

So, equipped with the batting gear (smartly dressed self- confident, ready to conquer the world) I stepped into the arena of the working world. Talk about being bowled? The run-up, bound coil release, follow through, I was blasted with all!

From *'No experience, Are you for real?' to 'Lady at your age, (44) seriously? You gotta have more than dress well, speak well!'* Dismissed by supercilious HR managers and having exhausted all my friendly connections my resolve, ego did take bowled out for zero, but then my tenacity and belief in myself was just too strong. I wasn't going to surrender to circumstances and no one was going to dictate what I could and would do except me. Was I going to allow myself to be bowled over again? Not in this lifetime!

I had been plunged in that boiling water of penury but was fast recovering from the scalding trauma. In retrospect all that was superfluous, the facades, the inauthenticity had been boiled away. I had stewed enough in self-pity and my essence of me, myself strong, distilled, fluid ready to spread MY flavour My message Me, emerged.

While I was in hot waters the intensity of the heat increased my faith in the Almighty, My Creator, The Universe call it what you may was restored and I prayed with full faith never doubting that this too would pass. Absolute Belief and Clear Intent.

My prayer was *'please just open a door for me to step in and I would do all in my power and will succeed'.* No what type of door just a door. And no matter how many times I was rejected I never questioned or complained my prayer never changed.

My prayers were answered in the form of an announcement in the classifieds (remember I was not 'experienced' or 'qualified' so I had stopped looking) but on that day in November 1996 my attention was drawn as the announcement was in a bold black border it read

'IF YOU ARE A PEOPLE'S PERSON AND, YOU THINK YOU HAVE GOOD COMMUNICATION SKILLS, NO EXPERIENCE REQUIRED TRAINING PROVIDED'.

I was so overwhelmed at this answer to my prayers I started crying – tears of gratitude, joy, relief. I went to the seminar with the attitude that job assignment was already mine I just had to show up... (déjà vu college) and that is exactly what happened. I attended the seminar posed some questions to the presenter, who is still my boss, at the end of the presentation, I along with 7 out of the 65 who attended was asked to stay back and with NO interview I was offered the job of a financial planning consultant!

Selling Life Insurance in the UAE in the 90s was a challenge! Selling life insurance is a tough way to make a living and an even more difficult way to sustain a lucrative, long-lasting career. Industry analysts place the burnout rate for first year at 90%! It was extremely difficult to know where to start. I was new in the country and had few leads. Even when I did locate good prospects, the product itself was hard to sell. People are averse to discuss or even acknowledge their own mortality. Moreover, unlike a new car, the latest smart phone or a trip to an exotic destination! Life insurance provides none of the instant gratifications that leads people to make impulse decisions and purchases.

Attitude, belief, courage/charisma, determination, and loads of energy important elements to my success. When people treated me with disdain, were rude, abrupt, angry I followed the advice of my boss: 'develop a thick skin don't let people's behaviour determine your attitude' I threw all qualms out of the window, I knocked on doors... Cold calling - I made countless phone calls, no matter how many rejections I never lost faith and the tide did turn in my favour. My income grew so did my knowledge, personal and professional development. I discovered facets of me that excited and energized me. The Universe did not just open a door it opened a gateway, a myriad of possibilities!

2000, a near death experience on the operating table gave me a new lease on life. I found myself on the path of self-discovery a trajectory that continues to this day ….. I rose from the immersion of self for others to Me for Me. I rediscovered my true self. I am in the driver's seat. I embarked on a voyage, an expedition of adventure, to spread my wings and fly…… skydiving, water rafting, mushing with the huskies in the Arctic circle, experiencing Ayahuasca in Peru to pilgrimages in Tibet walking at 18,500 feet I continue to seek out physical and mental challenges

2020 a year of cleansing of jettisoning the old. Things appear uncertain. As I write this account of my life I sit by my (87 year-old) mother's side. She suffered a stroke, we nearly lost her, my sister and I resuscitated her, a scary situation it was, the ambulance arrived in the nick of time. She is on the road to recovery, physiotherapy and more A resilient woman who had a challenging life but is full of love and has always been there for each of her children. Her tenacity, will power, her never give up attitude is what is taking her forward on her road to recovery and physical independence

Yet again, I find myself in an untenable position, I now have to reorganize my life change the way I do business reorganize my time and use my energies in a different yet efficient manner this time around I'm in total surrender, I'm not being Ms Fixit because it just doesn't work! I'm living in the 'present' and enjoying the 'gift' of now.

Relationships- yes, a big part of anyone's life, family, spouse, offspring, friends, business associates, I have had a 180-degree change in the way I approach everything. My spouse could not understand the 'new' me, he wanted me to get back to where I was, i.e. subservient and dependent. Well, each of us are free to be delusional.

Life experiences are one's best teacher and what it has taught me is that all the answers, the solutions lie within. I am tuned into my internal GPS my intuition, inner voice, my soul! That voice that prompter is never wrong! Unfortunately, we are conditioned to think 'logically' with our mind. I am learning to have faith in the wisdom that lies deep inside of me, for it knows me better than anyone else. I am responsible for me I cannot hold another accountable for my financial, emotional well-being.

Money, financial independence, taking/making decisions for my well-being, weighing the pros and cons, rejecting, amending reading the fine print this is now my way of watching out for me. If that offends others so be it. Financial independence gives you choices, dignity, respect and freedom to live life on my terms. No compromises

In essence my life be it successes or challenges has taught me

To be myself I'm am unique like my fingerprint!

The only constant in life is change

When my life is a battlefield I will fight boldly, even when the walls are crumbling around me and the earth is cracking beneath my feet, I will not expect or fear anything

Expectations and fears limit my possibilities

To be in Surrender

Stop being Ms Fix It

The root cause of our unhappiness depression, etc. is that we fail to understand the impermanence of things.

If I think I cannot accomplish a task, I am now in awareness that I have lost the battle before it has even started! So, I do not doubt myself as I am aware that I will not be able to do anything after that!

I consciously believe that I am capable enough of accomplishing any and every task that is allotted to me and I will succeed in the situation despite circumstances

My endeavour is to live in the NOW

Drop expectation and let go of the ego (trying hard!)

Practising – Drop the E and just GO

Yes, the dunking in the hot waters of penury helped my find my true flavour. My Attitude and Abilities, Beliefs and Courage and Charisma Determination, Faith, Energy and above all LOVE surfaced and I continue on my amazing, brimming with possibilities journey of LIFE

The Universe has Unquestionable ways. So, here's me Sandi Saksena having found my way from the teapot of financial ruin into the cups of possibilities to use/share my true-life experiences, the highs and the lows to help other become financially secure. I have and continue to spread my authentic, essence and flavour. Those whose lives I flavour with my work, my seminars, my writing my speaker engagements, TV, Radio are well on their paths to financial Security and Financial Independence. Emotionally Empowered!!

What Else is Possible How Can it get any better than this?

Amen

ABOUT THE AUTHOR

A Tor - accelerator, mentor negotiator, manipulator, motivator, facilitator, arbitrator, orator, commentator, conservator, invigorator, moderator, tutor… Yes, I'm All That And More. I offer all of the above to people who want more out of their lives… Money, career, relationships, health and wellness

A long-time resident of the Gulf, I have lived in Kuwait, Bahrain and now in Dubai for 5 decades. Circumstances pushed me to find a job, A late entrant into the work force age 44, with no previous work experience I could not even prepare a CV!

I devote my time and energies to my career in personal financial planning. I lead a team of financial consultants at Nexus Insurance Brokers, I head the division 'Family Matters' at Echelon Advisors and Management Consultants my family firm, and have recent launched my platform FIT an Empowerment initiative among other projects. I serve as advisor on various international women empowerment platforms.

I believe that building trust, and loyalty, sharing and giving, dealing with integrity and honesty are essential ingredients to success in both the personal and professional arena. Personal experiences and insurmountable challenges are your best teachers! They make your stronger and more resilient.

I am a regular contributor to the media on topics related to personal finance, Powerhouse Global Magazine edition all through 2020, Executive Women ME and a blog on World is One, WION, a popular well-respected international news channel

I am a frequent guest speaker on radio and TV and am frequently quoted in the business pages of the of local and international publications.

I am a speaker, moderator and host at International conferences / conventions. I am a mentor, my focus is Leadership, Relationships, Value of Self, Going with flow, Stay Relevant, and core focus - Financial Independence & Empowerment of Women.

W: www.echelonamc.com
Facebook: https://www.facebook.com/sandi.rich.7
https://twitter.com/sandisaksena
https://www.linkedin.com/in/sandi-rich-saksena-a9771593/

CHAPTER 14

MY FIGHT OF FREEDOM

NAOKO ITO

For others it is a beautiful thing to become an adult, but it was a different experience for me. My story has never been told publicly and writing this to share with the world is a new level of healing for me. We sometimes see people looking beautiful on the outside, but we don't realise what is going on in their inside. Women know how to cover up pain and distress and most times they get caught up in their own mess and it ends up destroying them. This story is to encourage anyone out there who is going through personal challenges. You may be thinking by now what is she talking about? What I'm about to share with you started almost 40 years ago. It is my personal story and it has taken me a lot of courage to put this out for others to draw strength from it. It took enough encouragement from my partner and loved ones to share this with the world. To some it seems easier, but for me it has not been a walk in the park. I never knew that one day I will be able to share this secret pain of mine.

What I will say to you at this point is to ask for help when you feel your life is not going in the right direction. In my case, I never asked for help and due to this mistake my life was almost ruined. During these years I lost good relationships as well as damaged some parts of my body. An addiction is something one cannot explain unless they come to a place of acceptance. I started fighting my demon (eating disorder) at the age of 19. I was afraid to add weight and nothing made sense to me during those years of fighting. The fear of eating and keeping the food in my system scared me, and it became my lifestyle until recently.

No member of my family was aware of this challenge I had to deal with all these years, but they only observed my high appetite to food. I could consume so much food in front of them, but it will end up in the toilet afterward. I was like an eating machine when I was with my family and friends. I even got complimented for my love of food even though I look as tiny as a size zero. No one took time to find out what was going on with me, so I carried on living the life of deceit by pretending to love food so much. It was my secret life for over 35 years. Even my late husband never found out about this secret. My stomach line finds it difficult to retain food due to the over stretch of my system.

Unfortunately a lot of girls suffer from this illness especially those in the modelling industry. They are forced to stay slim and they don't get much encouragement to stay healthy. Eating disorders are a common illness amongst girls because they are afraid to add any form of weight. In my case I didn't know any better because I had the notion that I was too fat, a notion that still lingers in some form today. Little did I realise that all these were in my head. Because I have been involved with this lifestyle for too long, it became a part of my daily habit. No matter how delicious a meal may taste, it must be forced out of my system after consuming it.

Most of my friends wish they could eat like me, but what they did not know is what happens to the food after consumption. It was a double life and it took so much energy to cover my tracks. After my vomit I had to wash the toilets to ensure no one finds out about my activities. Imagine the amount of toilet washing I had done in the last 35 years? Yes, it took me 35 years to step out of this lifestyle. 35 years of pain and erosions of my enamel due to the acid from my stomach. Too much vomiting has cost me my natural teeth and I have spent so much money fixing my teeth in the past 35 years. Not to even mention the food bill.

In those early years consuming food became an obsession. This was because in order to vomit I need a full stomach. Without that I felt vomiting would be too hard and would retain the food that I had just eaten. It was not unusual for me that after a nice restaurant meal I would buy takeaway on the way home just to be sure I had enough in my stomach to vomit.

This also caused relationship challenges, for example, a night out with family usually ended early because I wanted to go home and vomit. Leaving early caused many arguments with my husband. If not able to get home, vomiting in the toilets of trains, planes, restaurants where cleanliness standards varied was my alternative. Needless to say I always found a way.

When I turned 40 I started seeing some changes in my thinking. Although I was still engaging in the vomiting activities, but my hunger for such was reduced when I joined the swimming and yoga classes. I use to almost have a panic attack when I feel that fat is taking over my body. It was this psychological fear which takes over my mind once food goes into system that makes me vomit afterwards. Until recently, I never viewed my challenge as an illness. To me it was a way of living until I started talking about it to my partner who encourages me to jot down my thoughts and feeling. As I engage in these activities, the fear started diminishing and my confidence grew and now I am able to eat and keep the food in. writing this piece has taken me back to the place of my decision to diet at the age of 15. During those early years no one bothered about what others are doing, hence my family did not notice what I was doing. There was a period when I drank only milk to stay alive. I got used to starving myself of food for days just to lose weight. Never did it occur to me that one day I will be living a full life of 'eating disorder'. My struggle was the fear of being called 'fat'. I still believe that in our today's world a lot of women and young girls are living a similar life without anyone finding out about it. The danger of such lifestyle is the damages it causes in later life. And in this piece I will make some suggestions on how to deal with such dangerous commitment. I called it 'dangerous commitment' because vomiting food after consumption is a commitment to oneself not to allow food to stay in one's system. The most dangerous part of this commitment is the constant acid which damages one's enamel afterwards. To add to that, the risk of getting osteoarthritis was heightened along with other health challenges because on the continual loss of minerals due to the vomiting. When one is in that state nothing matters at all. All one thinks about is the activities which follows after the food goes into the system.

When my late husband was diagnosed with cancer and I had to look after him, I found myself not paying attention to my habit as much as I would have when I had lots of time on my hand. Taking care of him was all that mattered to me during the time of his illness until he sadly passed away. This left me broken and confused, but I managed to find strength to carry on with my life. In recent years I have become mindful of my behaviour to food and engaging actively in yoga has helped me tremendously to deal with my challenge. Also my partner's support has helped me to fight harder and to become a better person for myself and hopefully those whom my story would inspire to let go of such a habit.

In conclusion, I want to encourage anyone who is being challenged by this habit to get help as soon as possible. Don't delay it; just ask for help from the right people. I know this addiction carries with it shame and other negative feelings, but the more you learn to share it with trusted individuals, the easier you can deal with it, because you will have others who would hold you to accountable. And by putting it out there, you weaken the power of the illness. You see, this is what people do in the secret and the power of secret is stronger than the power of open confession and admittance. So many people go on the journey alone until it completely destroys their lives. I was one of those who thought I could do it on my own until my partner showed up. It was his encouragement that leads to the writing of this piece and by doing this, I feel stronger by the day and my previous fear has no hold over me again because someone is watching and encouraging me at the same time. Don't fight it alone – get help. My emphasis is on young girls who are afraid to add weight and those who want to look like dolls. Remember there are prices to pay for such desire, and those prices could even cost you your life. I want to tell you that you are absolutely beautiful the way you are. Don't allow society and the media to sell you images that are not yours. What you should be asking yourself when you feel like being unkind to your body are:

- What is the effect of what I'm doing to myself?
- Who is making me do this to myself?
- What are the benefits of these actions?
- Is this ok?
- Would a successful people do this to themselves?

These are some of the triggers of this habit:

*Emotional need – I lost my mum when I was 5 years old and this lead to my dad marrying another woman. It was difficult for me to deal with not having my mum around. I knew my dad loved me but it wasn't enough. As a little girl, my dream was to always wake up with my mother beside me. Imagine what I had to deal with during those years, and having another woman as a mother was not easy too. Although she tried her very best to make me and my brother comfortable but the thought of not having my mum played daily on my mind. So, I had to grow up quicker than I should have just to become my own decision maker.

* Lack of attention – This is one trigger of this habit. You sometimes see girls who feel left out when their friends are having more attention than they have. It arouses the thought in the mind of these girls. The question of: Are my not good enough? This can lead to negative habit formations which include eating disorder just to look slim.

* Change of environment – the fear of acceptance can also trigger negative habit. And it is the duty of adults to encourage their young ones to gradually integrate into the new system (environment). It requires constant reminder of how beautiful they are.

ABOUT THE AUTHOR

Born in Japan, Naoko Ito is a popular yoga instructor based in Singapore. She enjoys challenging people to be the healthiest version of themselves.

CHAPTER 15

AUSTRALIA – DREAMS, DECISIONS, DESTINATION

By, Vera Petrova

"You can, you should, and if you are brave enough to start, you will." Stephen King

My Childhood

I grew up in a small country Slovenia which is neighbour to Austria, Italy, Hungary and Croatia. My parents are by origin from Macedonia and when they got married they moved to Slovenia in the early 1970's. My Mum had a cousin there and she wanted to join her, however my Dad worked for a few years in Switzerland prior to meeting my Mum, and his wish was to move with the 'fresh marriage' to Switzerland, but Mum was not keen to go in that direction.

In early 1970's my only brother Saso was born. Four years later my parents gave life to me - the author of this short story.

I lived my childhood in lovely Slovenia, a country that is named as the green heart of Europe these days, has always been very beautiful, clean and peaceful. I was lucky enough to have a good education and classmates from primary school all the way up to various high schools that I completed, and friends from my University. On my educational path, I had the opportunity to meet brilliant people and some extraordinary teachers and professors who I keep in contact with till these days.

We can imagine that possibly every child might have a wish, a dream, for one day to become a reality. And yes, here it comes. My Dad has two sisters who emigrated to Australia around the time he was working in Switzerland. I remember as a child that we had a regular contact and communication with both my aunties in Australia and their families. I watched documentary programmes on the TV and read articles and books and even later learned at school about this beautiful continent – Australia. The thing I was most impressed with was the nature and animal beauty. This country has so much to offer for everyone, so it is easy to fall in love with it.

My wish was that one day I, my brother and parents could go on holiday or move to Australia. A situation came about when my Dad lost his job, so his oldest sister Stefka who lives in Brisbane, kindly offered and sent an emigration pack for us as a family to emigrate to Australia due to the current crisis as my Dad being without a job. My Dad was always prepared to take a risk, take another step in life, and accept a challenge as necessary, but my Mum is a bit different. She did not think we needed to make this move at that certain time and we continued living in Slovenia.

My first very well paid job

I worked in many different fields and one of my professions is a construction technician. When I got employed in early 1999, I started working on various giant construction – civil engineering projects then decided to save some money in order to travel to Australia. And it happened. My first visit to this exotic continent was conducted for two months. I had ideas where I wanted to go, what I wanted to see and overall to visit my relatives in Brisbane and Sydney. I recall this achievement as a 'miracle happens' in one's life! Seriously! I remember very well the travel agent on the day when I made the flight booking, the lady told me that whilst I was looking at my tickets that I looked as though I did not believe this was actually happening. And this is pure truth. My feelings were so real that I could not believe it that I was planning to take on this long journey.

Even these days I talk about how unbelievable it was to me that I had achieved my dreams. I visited the land that always impressed me so much when seeing it either on TV programmes, news or elsewhere. While on that trip I had a wonderful time, my brother and my partner travelled with me. We loved it - every second spending it in the nature, with the animals and having special quality time with our family.

We had a couple internal flights booked and visited places in Queensland, New South Wales, Victoria and Central Australia. Once on this journey, I also managed to visit New Zealand for 10 days.

Visa process

After I finished University, I started working in social work within the public and government sector. Later in 2007, I started the process to obtain a visa to emigrate to Australia as I was already qualified and after university with no other responsibility attached to me. The company and the founder who was doing the visa procedure seemed well experienced in the emigration process. As a part of the visa requirement, I passed the ELTS (English Language Test System). During that time I decided to visit Australia again for a good month, in order to make my mind clear as what I really want.

I travelled with my partner who was also keen to emigrate with me and consider, if we both thought that this was the right decision to do. Again, we really enjoyed every second being on this gorgeous continent, travelled around many territories and hiring vehicles on every airport that we landed, for the purpose of travelling long hours on the roads and discovering new areas. This time we even liked the weather more as it was in April and it was not that hot as it was the first time I visited the country in December and January.

However, revisiting and considering that dream as I always wanted 'down there, gave me some food for thoughts. Once I returned back home I did my pros and cons of living in Australia. I realised that if living in Europe I can travel more frequently and easily and stay close to my parents. On the other hand, emigrating to Australia could be much more difficult when it comes to travelling arrangements and also being on distance with my parents. Overall, I made a decision not to emigrate at that point as I considered a new opportunity because in between of the visa process I already started working and living in the United Kingdom.

Started working in the United Kingdom

In 2008 I started working in the UK. I have been practising as a Qualified Social Worker in many interesting and rewarding roles across the country. I cannot stress enough my appreciation and gratitude for everything I have experienced to date. I could and perhaps I can write serial chapters or books in the near future about various topics based on my life and experience.

Firstly I moved to South of England to the seaside in Brighton. I performed some jobs through the social care agency in the community and residential care setting. Parallel I started travelling to London and working for the Social Services. Mostly I covered weekend shifts in learning disability care homes in the south coast all around Brighton. Working for Social Services was quite different in comparison to the approach that I had experienced back home in Slovenia. There was no doubt that I enjoyed my work and moreover I was able to train and learn along the job that I was doing. And as I know myself, I always want to learn new things, challenge and better myself as this builds my confidence and fulfils my overall expectations.

Later on after about 2 years I decided to move to London to make my life easier in terms of travelling to work every day from Brighton to London. Some weekends I still travelled to work to do the shifts in the residential care homes at the seaside. In fact, I loved living in Brighton and London. I worked for one Local Authority in London for about 5 years which I honestly enjoyed the projects that I was involved with and the colleagues that I was lucky to meet there. I keep these friendships closely to myself.

As life goes on, at one certain time I was offered a job in Lincolnshire. I moved for a short couple of months to that area, working in Social Services. My professional life and career was going higher and I was offered to remain in the employment on a long term contract, however I decided to return to London. Here I had a numerous new posts and interviews for which I secured my job before returning from Lincoln.

My career path continued for some time in the capital of England then I made a new decision to purchase a property in East England and for that reason and my convenience I decided to get employed close by. I have been living and working in that part of the country and enjoyed my career progress more and more. During my working, travelling and other commitments I considered to undertake a course in Interior Design as I already have some background from my high school and have always enjoyed design in many different ways. I do not know what impresses me more fashion design – outfits or interior design – property dressing. Or honestly both! I completed college and obtained a diploma in interior design.

Lastly, when I look back at what I have been going through in my personal and professional life, it seems like a destiny. Life is full of making decisions, destinations and dreams come true. Right? But I think one has to take into consideration and include what actually brings the happiness and satisfaction on the personal level and make that dream or decision change the life.

As a result, my thought today is that I travelled to Australia for great exploring and having fun and I aim to revisit more times as it is so much to see and enjoy on that gorgeous continent.

My parents

However, going back to my parents. In 2019 my Dad was ill to the point that my Mum was unable to safely continue care for him due to his physical and mental health needs. In addition, my Mum suffers from her own poor health.

In my Dad's best interest I managed successfully to place him into a residential care home. Dad is now partly blind, has Diabetes and Dementia and he is wheelchair dependant.

My Mum is recovering from day to day illness and continues to live independently at home. I ensured to make home for my Mum comfortable therefore I renovated the property from A to Z in order to give her more comfort and possible new chapter in her life, since she has been tired by caring for my Dad. My Mum always loved living in this property for the last 35 years and she has never wanted to move away, so her dreams become true.

Otherwise, looking at my Dad's situation, I think he has missed his opportunity whilst he was capable and able to achieve his dreams; there were other factors present that he did not chase for his dreams to come true. I feel sorry for him and honestly believe that we only have one life and should never allow someone or something to stop us dreaming and achieving.

My parents are both in their early seventies and in fact I have been cutting this long story short to indicate that is crucial to do the things and get what you want before it is too late. My Dad always wanted to visit Australia too due to the country natural beauty and obviously to catch up with his sisters when he was still fit and capable to travel, however sadly, this fact lies that he could not achieve his dream.

This, my first ever published story, is dedicated to my creators Mum and Dad, with my thanksgiving to them for their unconditional love and for giving me this precious life. Now, it is up to me what I am going to do with it...

I can definitely share my satisfaction for both my parents at this stage in their lives. I am ensured that my Dad is safe and he gets the care he needs. I love the fact that my Mum is independent and enjoys her life whilst she continues to live in the community and socialise with her close friends and relatives.

I feel happy for both of them and wish more happy years to come their way, no matter their physical or mental condition.

In the final note below, I wish to share some thoughts from one wise, witty, wonderful woman who makes her living with words – writing books, teaching seminars, and giving keynote speeches at conferences – BJ Gallagher.

Making Difference - *Women's Legacy to the World*

"What do you want to be remembered for when you die? I love to ask people this question. Their answers tell me much about what they are up to in life.

I once had the opportunity to ask Steve Jobs, co-founder of Apple and creator of the Macintosh computer. His answer surprised me. He said, 'I want to be remembered as the best father in the whole world.' Not what I expected from a living legend – a brilliant man who is a leading pioneer in the technology revolution, and a marketing genius to boot!

If I were to ask you the same question, 'How do you want to be remembered when you die?' what would your answer be?

You do not have to be world – famous to make a difference in the world. Perhaps you are active in your community, or in your church or synagogue. Maybe you are involved in politics. Millions of women make difference by volunteering in hospitals, hospices, homeless shelters, and social services organizations. Maybe the difference you make is in the arts, with your music, writing, painting, sculpture, or other art form. Perhaps you are one of those angels known as teachers – who make a huge difference by educating our next generation of citizens. And maybe, like Steve Jobs, the difference you are most interested in making is within your own family.

The question is: What will be your legacy to the world?" BJ Gallagher

My views based on my personal story are as follows; being a leader in your family circle or in a professional environment stands that one must possess grit, honesty, integrity and empathy and all in all be prepared to listen, learn, lead and leave a legacy of Love.

Change can often be an uphill battle hence essentially I want to ask you a question where we are equal? The answer is simple. We all share the same time. Time is precious value. Are we at the right time and at the right place to make a difference? What would you do if you were to have more time? If you can buy more time, what would you do differently? In my case I know my answer straightaway – I would ensure that my Dad gets that holiday visa, flight tickets and my company aboard all the way down to our beautiful destination – Australia.

"I may not have gone where I intended to go, but I think I have ended up where I needed to be." Douglas Adams

"The important thing... is not how many years in your life, but how much life in your years!" Edward Stieglitz

ABOUT THE AUTHOR

Verica Petrova is a Master Research Assistant - Student at MBA programme in Leadership and Management. She is an Experienced Social Worker with a demonstrated history of working in the government administration industry. She is skilled in Public Sector, Adults & Child Welfare, Social Services, Performance Management and Case Management.

Verica holds an award in Education and Training and she has been organising and delivering various workshops, trainings, courses and drop in sessions for health and social care professionals and has been performing a range of children craft activities.

As a Social Work student, Verica participated in the humanitarian project in Asia – Sri Lanka and Maldives after the tsunami disaster. This work included a numerous distribution of support in the community, families and individuals. She has completed her social work research diploma in Cyprus and collaborated in the expert excursion in USA – Florida. Verica has been working as a children mentor in a couple primary schools and as a teacher in children summer camps in Croatia.

Her mission is to continue her well known and appreciated work and add more value when it comes to interior inspiration. Verica is an Interior Designer with her background experience as a Sign-painter and Construction Technician and she loves to help with the property design and development, room arrangements, furniture styling, paintings and paint decorations, wall papers, choosing and matching fabrics, rugs, soft materials and home accessories and much more.

Her motto is: "Do all things with Love and Love will come back to you."

For her Interior Design ideas, plans, work and inspirations please follow her on Instagram:

https://www.instagram.com/colours_bring_brilliance/

Other Social Media Platforms on LinkedIn and Facebook:

https://www.linkedin.com/in/vera-petrova-55a22b66

https://en-gb.facebook.com/verica.petrova.58

She can be contacted on e-mail:

vpetrova404@gmail.com

CHAPTER 16

GLOBAL VISIBILITY

By Anita Duckworth-Bradshaw

We are living in the Global village and those who are serious about enjoying the benefits are already making huge moves. The new age of "information overload", and the birth of social or the jet age of endless possibilities which has seen the increase of personal and business growth. Although, it brought with it divisions in relationships…. Yes! More people spend a good % of their time on the internet and face – to – face conversations are gradually fading away.

Taking my thoughts back to 31st December 1999 when the world was at her knees praying for the day to break. So many people thought the world would come to an end at the arrival of year 2000. It was scary to listen to the news and the conversation of the majority. There was fear in the atmosphere and a lot of businesses shut down due to the fear of the unknown. There were so many unanswered questioned from children and young adults at that time. One could smell the scent of fear in the atmosphere.

What would the new age bring to us asked many? What would happen should the world end at the wake of January 2000? I could sense fear in my environment especially in the camp of those with so much wealth and who had given little to the poor amongst them. Suddenly, people gave their lives to Christ and desired to make heaven. I laugh about it now because I can vividly picture that period. I was only just a young adult working towards a better future with lots of opportunities on the horizon. At that time, I was only two months into my new job in a multi-national company in Nigeria. Then I stopped and asked myself; why would the world end now that I have just started to live my life, earn my own money without others interfering with my choices. Why now?

Little did I realise that GLOBALIZATION has come to stay, and those who are ready to welcome it will benefit tremendously. Yes! It did arrive and the world did not end as joy filled the air with lots of celebration. The only thing most people failed to realise at that time is that the world had suddenly become smaller. We welcomed the new technological age where you can be wherever you desire to be with a click of a button on your system.

We are living in a Global Village and to enjoy the benefits, we must position ourselves and our businesses with the aim of becoming 'GLOBALLY VISIBLE'.

Here are some of the keys of GLOBAL VISIBILITY;

- Identify your purpose – most individuals are living on other's idea of who they should become. Due to this ignorance, they follow the trend of the society and end up getting lost in the crowd. They end up with people who are going nowhere. Like one of my mentors' would ask; what are you about in the world?

I ask you who is reading this piece the same question; what are you about in the world? Not wanting to confuse you with my question, it simply means; what is your purpose on earth? Considering the asked question, you would understand that we are all expected to be about something whilst on earth (living our individual calling).

Isn't it scary to know that only 1% vital few of the earth population are absolutely in charge of the other 99% of the wondering generality? This I read from books such as 'THE SECRET' and some of the books written by leaders in personal and professional development. To become Globally Visible, one must identify who one is and what gifts one has within them. It is finding out one's role in the field of play that can better one's life and that of others. Show me a person who is living his/her purpose and I will show you a person of success.

Without purpose driven living, one becomes a part of the 99% wondering generality. Purpose identification is the start of personal and professional development discoveries. Those who have the privilege of knowing their purpose effortlessly rides the high tide of life. They are usually very optimistic and they are not afraid of the changes happening around them. The purpose driven individuals are eager to break new grounds, support those who are struggling and improve their current situation. So I suggest to you to go on a purpose finding mission in order to become more than you already are. Do not limit yourself by living on other's ideas. It is time to step out of your comfort zone and work your way towards a successful living. Take risks on yourself and others. Stop waiting for validation from people who are not really interested in your future.

As a young adult, I knew my purpose was to become a life transformer and make a name for myself. Growing up in an environment where people did not mind what they become was not an easy ride. I made a choice not to settle with the rest of the crowd and follow in their belief. It was as if I was rebellious to the system but my future was more precious to me than the conclusion in the minds of those around me. I could not settle with the crowd. I just did not see myself living a pitiable life. I was on a mission to succeed and to take others along with me. Some even doubted my motives of wanting to become more. I gave myself to reading and meditation. With God's help and my internal knowledge of who I am, I discovered courage. This became my daily companion to keep on pressing forward until I become the person I desired to be. I made conscious effort to edge towards my destination ignoring all the distractions along the way. You too can rise above your challenged situation by deciding to win. It is true that TOUGH ROADS CREATE

TOUGH PEOPLE. I am a product of tough roads and it will get better as I continue to work on myself.

- Have a clear-cut vision of the changes you desire in your personal and professional life. With vision comes motivation and direction. For one to begin a journey of any kind, one must know where one is headed for.

  Most people and businesses fail because of lack of vision. To become globally visible, one must identify where and when one wants to be seen or gain connections. The importance of having a vision before you commence on any project, is that you will be able to switch lanes or make a U-turn, when you discover that what you are seeing on your path, does not look like what you have envisioned before starting your journey. It helps one to make a quick correction before it's too late.

  Take a project for instance, before a good project is handed to a project Director and manager, the stake holders must have had a clear vision of what their product will look like during the time of commissioning (finished product). The project manager knows that stage boundary (monitoring stages of the project) had to be put in place before the project commences.

  The reason for having a stage boundary is to monitor the progress of the project, and to ensure that the workers are following the exact model of the project. The stage boundary helps to correct any errors on the project during the process of completion. If not corrected, it can lead to project rejection and could eventually cost more than the stipulated cost.

  Having a vision creates the opportunity of stage boundary in one's personal and professional life. This supports with changing directions at the right time and moving forward with confidence. There are times in our journey when it looks like nothing is working, even with all the effort we have made in our personal and professional work. At this point in our journey, it would be wise to remind ourselves of the vision we saw before setting out on that particular journey. Sadly, so many people have allowed others to twat their original vision because of sentiments and fear of rejection. Please stay on track with what you are called to do in this life. It is ok if you make mistakes or are rejected by those whom you thought would stand by your side until you have made it safely to you desired destination.

"To get somewhere meaningful, you must learn to drop a lot of baggage." – Anita Duckworth-Bradshaw

- Set Goals: To become Globally Visible you must prepare to set goals that would take you from where you are to a high ground in the field of play. Goal setters are world changers and they are not easily put off by the challenges life presents to them. Goals setting are the reason the 1% Vital few of the society are able to control the wealth of the Globe. When you have a goal, life become more interesting to live and the fear of failure diminishes.

Any individual without goals is simply leaving their lives to chances. Setting goals is not wishful thinking but a catalyst to facilitate the process of change. When you set a goal(s), you immediately align yourself with the endless possibilities that life has to offer. Until I understood this truth, I was one of the 99% wondering generality who thought that things just happen.

- Hold onto courage - Courage they say is the backbone of every successful individual. An individual with courage has the confidence to face any obstacle in life. As a powerhouse your courage will see you through every challenge that comes your way. Apparently, the lack of courage creates problems and difficult living in the lives of so many people.

Those who made history in their time had courage – no wonder a great philosopher said;

"Courage does not always roar. Sometimes courage is the quiet voice at the end of the day saying, "I will try again tomorrow." – Mary Anne Radmacher

It does not matter what you may have been through – hold onto courage and she will sail you safely to your desired destination. When you embrace courage you will see possibilities in every challenge you are faced with. It took courage to leave my native land (Nigeria) to Europe. It took courage to start my business. It also took courage to de-clutter my circle of influence, and to step away from those who no longer serve my purpose. Courage will take you to places you have never imagined before.

As a teenager, growing up in a very challenging environment made me stronger than my peers. I never celebrated birthdays until my 20th – then I had moved on and grown into my own person. Courage was the backbone of my ever increasing learning and evolution. The courage to succeed in my chosen areas of life was my source of strength. If you carefully study the lives of all successful people (women especially), you will discover that courage played an active part in their achievements.

How many times have you tried to work on your dreams? How many times have you allowed fear to get the better of you? A person without courage unconsciously invites weakening and demoralizing elements to themselves. Courage has the power to challenge all unfavourable situations. When you make courage your backbone, you will be able to face all physical, emotional, spiritual and mental battles of life.

Welcome to the best day of your life. Congratulations!

ABOUT THE AUTHOR

Anita Duckworth-Bradshaw (popularly known as Lady Anita Bradshaw) is the founder of Powerhouse Global Women organisation. She is an accredited life coach, a published author of 7 other personal development books. Lady Anita is the propagator of Powerhouse Global Brand (Powerhouse Global Awards, Powerhouse Global Academy, Powerhouse Global Magazine, Powerhouse Global Network and Powerhouse Global Leadership Conferences). She is a Global change agent with multi awards in her collections. She is also the President of Powerful Women Global Foundation Nigeria. Her charity supports women and children from deprived areas… She is a sought-after Global speaker.

As a personal development expert, her daily uplifting practice is to discover new ways of becoming, doing and having more through my work.

"I discovered a long time ago that a tree does not make a forest neither does a person make a market. Also, to achieve the forest or the market state we most collaborate with others."- Anita Duckworth-Bradshaw

www.powerhouseglobalwomen.com
www.powerhouseglobalmag.com

Lightning Source UK Ltd.
Milton Keynes UK
UKHW010824110920
369735UK00001B/11